KEEP "COMPANY" WITH GOD

7 Spiritual Principles
For Starting A
Successful Business
In The Kingdom Of God

Elder Carla A. Nelson

Foreword By
Dr. Myles E. Munroe

PRESS

KEEP "COMPANY" WITH GOD

7 Spiritual Principles
For Starting A
Successful Business
In The Kingdom Of God

Elder Carla A. Nelson

Keep "Company" With God, LLC

Lanham, Maryland

Editorial Note:
Even at the cost of violating grammatical rules, I have chosen:
1. To capitalize *He, Him, His* when referring to God or Jesus.
2. To capitalize the word *Will*, when referring to God's Will.
3. To refer to Holy Spirit as a person, not a thing, therefore you will not see "the Holy Spirit".
4. Not to capitalize the name satan and related names.

Scripture quotations noted **KJV** is from *The Thompson Chain-Reference Bible King James Version, copyright 1998.*

Scripture quotations noted ***The Message*** is from *The Message: The Bible In Contemporary Language, by Eugene H. Peterson.* Copyright 1993, 1994, 1995, 1996, 2000, 2001, 2002. Used by permission of NavPress Publishing Group.

"Used by permission of Thomas Nelson, Inc." – non-exclusive English language only. This printing only.

Word definitions noted ***M-W***: By permission. From ***Merriam-Webster Online Dictionary*** © **2003** by Merriam-Webster, Incorporated (www.Merriam-Webster.com).

Information by Dr. Ira V. Hilliard is used by permission.

Information by Dr. Myles E. Munroe is used by permission.

Information by Dr. Charles Phillips is used by permission.

Xulon Press
www.XulonPress.com

Xulon Press books are available in bookstores everywhere, and on the Web at www.XulonPress.com.

Cover Design:
Ms. Shalonda Moses – *By The Spirit* bytheSpirit27@aol.com

Photograph:
©Brathwaite Photography www.brathwaitephoto.com

KEEP "COMPANY" WITH GOD

Keep "Company" With God, LLC
PO Box 1038
Lanham, MD 20703-1038
www.KeepCompanyWithGod.com

Sherry Soules

Enjoy reading my heart!

This Book is Dedicated to

Every Person Who Is Pregnant With A Desire
To Start Their Own Business And Is
Looking For Someone To Help Them
Push It Into Reality!

Carla A Nelson

12/12/04

"There is no greater assignment given to mankind than that of dominion over the earth. This mandate was given to man by his creator as the principle purpose of his creation. The very word **dominate** implies the need to govern, rule, to control, and to manage. In essence, the primary purpose for man's creation was to serve as manager of planet earth and its resources.

This heavenly mandate places management as the standard of judgment by the creator. You could say that the fall of mankind was the manifestation of mismanagement. Adam neglected his responsibility to look after the Garden under his care and forfeited the benefit of management.

With this understanding it is therefore understood that the fundamental role of man is to administrate the business of heaven on earth. Business is the very nature of mans' calling.

This is why Jesus states in Luke 16 that management will be the basis of God's judgment on mankind; how we use the resources we have been given.

In this work, ***Keep "Company" With God***, Elder Nelson takes us back to the foundational principle that no man manages God's resources without God's influence and in keeping with His precepts. I believe this book will be a great asset to anyone who desires to succeed in business under the principles of the Word of God. This book will be a classic and should be read by every young entrepreneur who has a vision for a successful enterprise. I encourage you to read the following pages and experience a higher level of business ethics and wisdom".

Dr. Myles E. Munroe

Bahamas Faith Ministries International
Nassau, Bahamas

The invention of jobs is a relatively recent concept of just over one hundred years ago with the introduction of the industrial revolution. Prior to that all business was conducted based on trade and bartering.

We see very early in the Bible that when God introduced Adam to this phenomenon in the Garden of Eden he told him to "dress it and keep it". This means he was not only responsible for acquisition but for maintenance of the garden. Being fruitful and multiplying are notions that were in the mind of God from the start.

I believe there is far more hidden potential inside of people than they realize. God placed everything on the planet with it's potential already inside. That's why a bird never goes to flight school but they do fly. Fish never go to swimming school but they swim. I do not believe it is any different with humans. I believe there are many businesses and inventions waiting to be birthed. The world is waiting on what you are pregnant with. No job is designed to make you rich. People don't hire you to make you rich; they hire you to make *them* rich. Statistics confirm that real wealth does not come from working for someone else.

I have known Carla A. Nelson for many years and can attest to the fact that she has written from her passion and experiences. The premise of this book *Keep "Company" With God* is for starting your business with Kingdom principles from the Bible is rather a unique idea but I believe it is an idea whose time has come.

Your personal life assignment can very well be your business. You can't make money where you don't have talent and gifts. Your uniqueness can be package and offered to the world thru the "Company" you were designed to birth. This book will show you how. The only thing left is to *DO IT!*

Dr. Charles Phillips, Pastor

Kingdom Christian Center Church International
Washington, DC

INTRODUCTION

Delight thyself also in the Lord; and he shall give thee the desires of thine heart. Commit thy ways unto the Lord, trust also in him, and he shall bring it to pass. He shall bring forth thy righteousness as the light, and thy judgment as the noonday.

Psalms 37:4-6 KJV

This book comes from a *passion* to give the people of God the *right way* of developing a plan to start their business; the way God would have it developed. As a person who has the desire to build their company on Godly principles, you will gain knowledge of how to put *His Will* first in all you do *spiritually, emotionally and financially*, when you are in the marketplace.

It should be noted that people primarily start a business for four reasons:
1. *To Increase their Wealth*
2. *To Limit their Liability*
3. *To Protect their Assets*
4. *To Pass their Assets on to the next Generation*

There are many business books in Christian and mainstream bookstores that talk about Godly ethics, principles, operations and transactions, but I have not found one that speaks to people who have a vision to *start a business* with God, *to keep "company"* with Him. Seeing none, the burden to write one began inside of me. This book is a compilation of many ideas, principles and values. My resources are:

▼ *Biblical References from* **The King James Version and The Message Translation** *of the Bible.*
▼ *Quotes from ministers of the gospel of Jesus Christ*
▼ *Advice from Business Coaches*
▼ *Conversations with Business Colleagues, Friends and Authors*
▼ *Business Resource Guides I've read, But most of all*
▼ **The School of Hard Knocks** – *living in the world of business and procrastinating on responding to its challenges when Jesus was constantly trying to show me the right way!!!*

The *7 Spiritual Principles* for starting your successful business in the Kingdom of God are

> 1. *Purpose & Vision: The Perfect Tag Team*
> 2. *Faith & Prayer: Building A Firm Foundation*
> 3. *Just Be…A Season of Preparation*
> 4. *YOU Are The Business*
> 5. *Get Dressed For The Day*
> 6. *Counting The Costs*
> 7. *Business Fundamentals: Write the Vision Down*

These seven principles are designed to assist you in the development of starting your business. This book is meant to be a resource and a guide for kingdom citizens who want to start and *keep a "Company" with God.* You need to know that you are not crazy, impractical or being unrealistic. Many times external forces will tell you to do things one way but your inner man is telling you to do it a different and sometimes awkward way. It doesn't mean that the world's way is wrong; it just means it might not be the *RIGHT WAY* for you! The Message Bible says it this way:

Get insurance with God and do a good deed, settle down and stick to your last. Keep company with God, get in on the best. Open up before God, keep nothing back; he'll do whatever needs to be done: He'll validate your life in the clear light of day and stamp you with approval at high noon.
Psalms 37:4-6 The Message

This passage of scripture also tells us to keep company or open communication with God as you go through life. Getting His input in everything you do because it is He who leads and guides you in the right direction. To *keep company,* in the Greek language is to *Kollao* (Cleave). It is to *join himself, in a sense of becoming associated with a person so as to company with him, to join fast together, or to be on his side.*

Keep in mind that starting a business is at least a five-year process! You will have successes as well as disappointments. This is all part of the process in order to become complete, entire and wanting nothing. God has already given you the reward you are seeking. God has already purposed your life to be one of success and to have a successful company! It is now your time to begin the journey.

TABLE OF CONTENTS

SPIRITUAL PRINCIPLE #1
Purpose & Vision: The Perfect Tag Team (You can't have one without the other)

---

*To find your purpose is to find your Life. Once you find your purpose you
must pursue it.
Your purpose will depress you if you don't.
Your purpose in life is not to go to work everyday and do
something for a paycheck;
That is your Job!
Your purpose is your true work (passion), and your true work
you will do for FREE"*

Dr. Myles Munroe

PURPOSE

BIBLICAL REFERENCES:
*Remember this, and show yourselves men: bring it again to mind, O ye trans-
gressors. Remember the former things of old: for I am God, and there is none
else; I am God, and there is none like me, Declaring the end from the beginning, and from ancient times the things that are not yet done, saying, My counsel shall stand, and I will do all my pleasure: Calling a ravenous bird from the
east, the man that executeth my counsel from a far country: yea, I have spoken
it, I will also bring it to pass; I have purposed it, I will also do it.*

Isaiah 46:8-11 KJV

*And we know that all things work together for good to them that love God, to
them who are the called according to his purpose. For whom he did foreknow,
he also did predestinate to be conformed to the image of his Son, that he might
be the firstborn among many brethren. Moreover whom he did predestinate,
them he also called: and whom he called, them he also justified: and whom he
justified, them he also glorified. What shall we then say to these things? If God
be for us, who can be against us? He that spared not his own Son, but delivered
him up for us all, how shall he not with him also freely give us all things? Who
shall lay any thing to the charge of God's elect? It is God that justifieth.*

Romans 8:28-34 KJV

I believe God has a mission. The entire mission of His life (eternity)
is to get His *purpose* done in the earth. Since God created time, the
earth, and man, He is in no rush to complete it, and the word failure
is not in His vocabulary. As Dr. Charles Phillips says, *"God does*

not play nine inning games, He just plays until He wins". God designed *purpose* in each and every one of us.

We define *Purpose* as *something set up as an object or end to be attained; intention; resolution; determination; a subject under discussion or an action in course of execution; or to purpose as an aim to oneself.*

In order for God's Will to be accomplished in the earth, He needs man – human beings – you and me to do the work! So often we are taught in the church that His Will is relegated to preaching from the pulpit, teaching in Sunday school, healing the sick and shut-in, doing mission work, and fellowshipping with the Saints. I would like you to think outside the box with me and apply God's Will in business:

SPIRITUAL	SECULAR
Ministering	*Business Consultation*
Pastor/Teacher	*Business Mentor or Coach*
Healing the Sick and Shut-in	*Getting your business out of crisis mode (usually short on resources)*
Mission Work	*Business Seminars, Classes & Workshops*
Fellowshipping with the Saints	*Networking with Business Owners, Companies, and yes – Churches!*

All business is God's business. If it is illegal or immoral, it is God's business corrupted, just like satan corrupts God's word and His people. It is through implementing a successful business idea that problems are solved and questions are answered, voids are filled, and needs are met. Every problem is a business waiting to be birthed. Who or what is to say that your business idea is not God's *purpose* planted inside of you waiting to be identified, written down, and actualized or manifested? You are the only one who can prevent God's *purpose* from being actualized in your life.

Consider this, since the *purpose* God planned to get done in the earth has to be done by man through business and commerce in the world, that man (male or female) might as well be you! As you live out your *purpose* you become the problem solver. People will seek you out for answers and pay you for it. Whether it is a service or product, it is a need that must be met. This is what we call business! As you become the problem solver, you will become well known and respected. Your reputation will be praised in the gates (a place where goods and services are sold. Legal matters conducted, and a symbol of power and authority as in Ruth 4:11). This is the process of prosperity.

This book of the law shall not depart out of thy mouth; but thou shalt meditate therein day and night, that thou mayest observe to do according to all that is written therein: for then thou shalt make thy way prosperous, and then thou shalt have good success.

Joshua 1:8 KJV

God gives each of us a *purpose* for being on this earth. It is your task, responsibility, or duty to find out what your *purpose* is, and complete it successfully before you depart this earth. I believe to do anything less is a sin (falling short of God's Will for our lives). Dr. Myles Munroe gives scriptural meaning to *purpose* as *the key to fulfillment; to live to your maximum potential; full of determination; having a purpose or aim; meaningful; it will make your enemies your staff; and, God will use everything to fulfill His purpose.* As a citizen of the Kingdom of God and to be in business for yourself it is important that you don't forsake your righteousness (standing in right position with God) just to make a 'quick buck'. God wants you to have a fulfilled life, a life that brings success and prosperity in all that we do because:

▼ *You make God look good to those who don't know Him*
▼ *You verify that His work is true to those who believe in Him*
▼ *God's word (the Bible) says so*

People who lead a life of *purpose* do not die prematurely. *Purpose* minded people die empty leaving no idea in the grave. Decide today to be a person of *purpose*. A person that has something set up to be attained. Be determined with a firm resolve to birth the solution to the world's problem, no matter how big or how small. Be a person who is willing to complete their reason (*purpose*) for being born.

Purpose leaves a mark for others to see. It is eternal and will live after you die. Instead of your life being marked by a big tombstone with the inscription of your life in the cemetery, the inscription for your life will be the beneficial mark you left in the earth. A mark that continues to help others live a better life even when your life is finished. Now that is what I call a Living Testimony!

> *Death respects Purpose.*
> *If you are fulfilling your purpose in life, you cannot die until you are finished.*
> *Just look at the life of Moses, Joseph, Daniel, Jesus, and Paul.*
> *Dr. Myles Munroe*

One of the hardest things I had to come to grips with was that in order to please God, I had to do *His Will.* As a pre-teen, I was taught or told by some Churchians that the things comprised of doing His Will made for a boring life. All the fun was taken away – no dancing, going to parties or socials (unless they were at church), no talking or don't be so loud when talking (especially for girls), and most of all, it is not considered 'Christian-like' to voice your own opinion! Voicing my opinion was the one thing I wanted to do most!

It wasn't until I was grown (or at least thought I was), dropped out of college, divorced, working two jobs, and starting all over again that I came to a church that taught me the *true* meaning of God's Will. *I am willing to expose the tough parts of my life because you need to know that no one lives the perfect life and it was not always easy for me.* I learned that God's Will was for me to fulfill *my purpose* in life that He set *in me* before I was born, just like Jeremiah (see Jeremiah 1:4-10). The vision I had in April 1992 confirmed the very reason why I was created and the *way* I was created. Remember God does not make mistakes and He does not quit on us! I realized that to allow God's Will in my life would give me the most pleasure because it would be to live my life as fulfilled as I wanted and the way God planned it. To live to my maximum potential!

I learned that my *purpose* included all those things I was told I should not do if I were to be a *good Christian*. In my business, I have a reputation of putting on the best parties and socials:

▼ *Networking Events*
▼ *Public Relations*
▼ *Fundraisers*
▼ *Event Planning*

When I was young, my best girl-friend's older sister said "Carla, you talk an awful lot," I said "yeah, and when I have something to say you guys usually listen. When I grow up, my mouth is going to make money for me"! At that time I had no idea how it would or if it could; the words just came out of my mouth. Today in my business, my mouth makes money for me through:

▼ *Business Consultation*
▼ *Ministering*
▼ *Speaking Engagements*
▼ *Training*

Through these channels of communications, I am able to do the one thing that gives me the most pleasure (and always tempered by Holy Spirit):

▼ *Voice My Opinion*
▼ *Negotiate (I can see both sides of a situation)*
▼ *Debate (the healthy ones)*
▼ *Influence others to make wise decisions*

The best part of all is that people listen to what I have to say and I get PAID to say it! Remember that *purpose* is constant. You were born with *purpose* in you therefore it cannot be changed. Your plans may change (how you complete your *purpose*) but your reason for being remains the same.

God does not change His rules to accommodate my ordeals,
I need to change my life to live by His ideas.
Dr. Cheryl A. Phillips

You can never become who you are until you identify who you really are. One way to identify the real you is to look at yourself and ask what are the things in life that grieve you the most? Whatever grieves you is the very thing you are designed to heal (design, improve, solve or correct). Again I say, to every problem there is a solution and from that solution a business can be birthed.

Here is a note for those of you who still work for someone else. Your ideas can be an improvement for the company for whom you work. Your solutions to the company's problems can result in a promotion. Remember God is the one who promotes. Whether it is directly from your employer, you leaving and getting a better job from another company, or starting your own business, all promotions are from God.

My mother would tell me when I was doing household chores to 'Do it right the first time so you won't have to repeat it'. I have come to learn that this saying holds true not only for household chores, but also in education, work assignments, church projects, and in relationships. Learn from the things that you go through on your job the first time around for you'll need them later in life. Every position you held in your work life in the past (and present), with all the duties, responsibilities, and assignments given to you will prove to be useful when you embark in your business. The knowledge you obtain through formal and informal education and the experience you gain from past relationships will all work together for your good because it is a necessary part of your *purpose.*

BIBLICAL REFERENCES:
Think about this. Wrap your minds around it. This is serious business, rebels. Take it to heart. Remember your history, your long history. I am God, the only God you've had or ever will have-incomparable, irreplaceable-From the beginning telling you what the end will be, All along letting you in on what is going

to happen, Assuring you, I'm in this for the long haul, I'll do exactly what I set out to do. Calling the eagle Cyrus, out of the east, from a far country the man I chose to help me. I've said it, and I'll most Certainly do it. I've planned it, so it is as good as done.

Isaiah 46:8-11 The Message

He (Holy Spirit) knows us far better than we know ourselves, knows our pregnant condition, and keeps us present before God. That's why we can be so sure that every detail in our lives of love for God is worked into something good. God knew what he was doing from the very beginning. He decided from the outset to shape the lives of those who love him along the same lines as the life of his Son. The Son stands first in line the line of humanity he restored. We see the original and the intended shape of our lives there in him. After God made that decision of what his children should be like, he followed it up by calling people by name. After he called them by name, he set them on a solid basis with himself. And then, after getting them established, he stayed with them to the end, gloriously completing what he had begun. So, what do you think? With God on our side like this, how can we lose? If God didn't hesitate to put everything on the line for us, embracing our condition and exposing himself to the worst by sending his own Son, is there anything else he wouldn't gladly and freely do for us?

Romans 8:28-34 The Message

Purpose is the key to your life's plan.
It answers the question
"Why was I born"?
and
"What is my reason for living"?

Carla A. Nelson

PURPOSE QUESTIONS:

1. When you were young, what did you want to be when you grew up? (Why were you born?) What was it that you wanted to:

   ▼ **Accomplish**
   ▼ **Become**
   ▼ **Improve**
   ▼ **Invest**
   ▼ **Solve**

2. Are you doing what it takes to complete this idea (*purpose*)? Have you achieved your *purpose* in life?

3. What will it take to begin or complete your *purpose* in life?

4. What is preventing you from fulfilling your *purpose* in life?

SPIRITUAL PRINCIPLE #1
Purpose & Vision: The Perfect Tag Team (You can't have one without the other)

EVERY DELAY IS NOT A DENIAL.
Just because somebody said NO today,
Does not mean they will say NO tomorrow.

Dr. Charles Phillips

VISION

BIBLICAL REFERENCE:
I will stand upon my watch and set me upon the tower, and will watch to see what he will say unto me, and what I shall answer when I am reproved. And the Lord answered me and said, "Write the vision, and make it plain upon tables, that he may run that readeth it. For the vision is yet for an appointed time, but at the end it shall speak, and not lie, though it tarry, wait for it; because it will surely come, it will not tarry".

Habakkuk 2:1-3 KJV

Blessed is the people that know the joyful sound: they shall walk, O LORD, in the light of thy countenance. In thy name shall they rejoice all the day: and in thy righteousness shall they be exalted. For thou art the glory of their strength: and in thy favour our horn shall be exalted. For the LORD is our defence; and the Holy One of Israel is our king. Then thou spakest in vision to thy holy one, and saidst, I have laid help upon one that is mighty; I have exalted one chosen out of the people.

Psalm 89:15-19 KJV

In the beginning my *vision* was such a burden to me because I did not understand what it meant. Since it involved my Pastor (who at the time was a minister at our former church), I asked him what it meant. He did not have a clue! His wife, Rev. Cheryl, said "God will reveal it to you in time". "*In Time?* I don't need to know *in time,* I need to *know NOW"!* (Yes, I also needed patience, but that comes later).

To get a better understanding of what was happening to me, the first thing I did was look up the word *vision* in the dictionary. *Vision* is *to see; something seen in a dream, trance or ecstasy; a supernatural appearance that conveys a revelation; an object of imagination; a manifestation to the senses of something immaterial; the act or power of imagination; a mode of seeing or conceiving; the unusual discernment or foresight; a direct mystical awareness of the super-natural usually in visible form; the act or power of seeing; or the special sense by which the qualities of an object constituting its appearance are perceived and which is meditated by the eye.*

Next I went to the Bible to search for the word *Vision. Vision* is found in the Bible 79 times in 73 verses, and *visions* is found 24 times in 24 verses. I listened to spiritual tapes and learned that God's greatest gift to man is *vision* for it is a source of hope. A person with *vision* is narrow-minded; all they can think about is fulfilling their *vision*. A true *vision* is like dreaming with God for His *visions* are:

▼ *A Natural Desire* – something you want to develop, invest, accomplish or solve to improve people socially, spiritually, economically, educationally or physically.

▼ *What Inspires You The Most* – what could you keep doing and not care about getting paid for. If your natural needs were met you would do it for free.

▼ *Designed To Help* - other people, a sense of mission to positively affect your society, or enhance the lives of others. It is not selfish or for vainglory. It inspires others and improves human life.

▼ *Connects With Your Love*– it is your passion, your motivator, your propeller, your reason to get up in the morning; your true desire. It is the right thing for the right reason in the right way.

Within 60 days God did reveal what His plan was for my life and what the company name would be. When your purpose is revealed to you and you begin to *see* the *vision*, the first thing you must do is... *Write the Vision Down* and name the *vision* (company). The name of my company became *Visionary Network Consultants*.

Visionary – the first word because my purpose was revealed to me in a vision.

Network – what I do between businesses and people.

Consultants - the way in which I provide service to my clients and customers.

Our tag line is *"Creating a Network for Businesses and Resources"* because the company foundation is built on networking people. I started marketing the company with this principle and use the 'Word of Mouth - Referral' technique to work for me. Remember I love to talk! Now Visionary Network Consultants, Inc. is the premier network and referral service company in the Washington Metropolitan area and my reputation is known in the gates as *Ms. Networker.*

Even though most people use the dictionary to obtain the proper meaning of words, sometimes it does not do you justice, therefore, I suggest you also use the Bible as your original resource and let the dictionary back up the Bible meaning. For example the dictionary defines *Visionary* as a *dreamer; one who is dreamy; illusory; imaginary or impracticable; a seer; utopian or unreal.* Yet the Bible states that a *Visionary* is one who has sight into the future, one who goes before, a forerunner, and a leader that prepares others. Examples of visionary people in the Bible are Joseph, Moses, Joshua, Daniel, John the Baptist, and Paul just to name a few.

In early 1993 I received a letter from a man who assisted me with starting my business idea that indicated some of these same words found in the dictionary about the word *visionary*. The letter said he hoped I was not dreaming or being unrealistic, because the thing I wanted to do did not seem like it would be profitable enterprise. By October 1996 I opened my first office, a meeting and training facility to be exact, because I stuck to my *vision.* He was there and had helped me make my dream a reality during those three years of preparation. He has been a big supporter by referring people to me and has been a fan of mine ever since!

The Bible indicates that those who dream are also capable of interpreting dreams and see the future (the unseen). Two of God's servants that accomplished their purpose in dream interpretation were Joseph and Daniel. You can't get any better than these two men of God. I decided that I would learn as much as I could about these two men and about having *vision* for my company. Let's look at the life of Joseph. He knew where he was supposed to be (his dreams) therefore, all the trials he went through were not permanent. When you see the end, you know when you are finished and you know when you are not!

In Genesis chapter 37, Joseph dreamed how the binded sheaves of his brothers made obeisance to his sheaf. His second dream was how the sun, moon, and eleven stars (representing his parents & eleven brothers) also made obeisance to him. Needless to say his family – albeit, his brothers were furious at him! How dare the youngest brother (and most beloved of their father) indicate that they would be taking orders from him. In today's terms it would sound something like this:

'Boy who the heck do you think you are? You're just a kid, what do you know? You got the audacity to stand there and tell us we are going to be working and paying homage to YOU. Hah! Likely story! You're just a spoiled brat. Dad lets you get away with anything and now it's gone to your head. You better hurry up and get outta' here before we hurt you'!

We've come to learn that Joseph and his dreams (*visions*) were a gift from God and he had a **natural desire** to help other people. He was great at managing

▼ *Resources*	*Genesis 39:2-5*
▼ *People*	*Genesis 39:21-23*
▼ *Money*	*Genesis 41:39-43*

His gift was something that **inspired him**. It was the "thing that turned him on". He definitely did not get paid for it because he was a slave. Joseph went from a child to a slave to a prisoner to a ruler.

The solutions Joseph gave when he interpreted dreams were always to ***help others***, never himself. His dreams made others rich, saved their life, and gave them food to eat during a time of famine. The only time Joseph asked for help was when he interpreted the dream for the chief butler to remember him when he went back to serve Pharaoh. The chief butler did – 13 years later!

Joseph's dreams ***connected with his true love***, the love of God and to serve God. God was his true motivator and heart's desire (he was enslaved and jailed without just cause)! He would sacrifice himself first rather than go against God's word, (he was tempted by Potipher's wife). He always did the right thing for the right reasons – even at his own expense.

I bought every book I could find on *vision, visions* and *visionary* people, but most of all I listened to the tapes and read the books of Dr. Myles Munroe, Pastor and founder of Bahamas Faith Ministries International. I call him the "Godfather of *Vision*". At least 90 % of what I know about vision comes from him and it is this knowledge I use to apply to the world of business to bless others. Dr. Munroe defines *Vision* as a *coming into being; the ability to see the end from the beginning; it is bigger than your life; it regulates your life because it is your reason for living; Vision is buried in Purpose. It is purpose exposed. It is a glimpse of your end and speaks of the end; it sets goals that motivate a plan of action; a mental representation of external objects or sense as in sleep; a conception in the imagination, mental image; and the ability to perceive, discern, and anticipate; foresight.*

Vision allows you to get excited about your business idea, so excited you cannot imagine quitting. Quitting is a word that should not found be in your vocabulary! All of us have eyes to see but not all of us can see *vision*. A blind man cannot see but he can see *vision*. God gives you an eye with the ability of *vision*. When your *vision* becomes clear it will:

▼ **Burden You** - If you do not pursue your *vision*, it will depress you because you are not doing what you were born to do. Nothing else in life will satisfy you. There will always be a void in your life as though something is missing but you can't figure out what it is. If you find yourself continuously talking about a problem that needs to be solved (the need to find good homes for hard to adopt children) or a situation that needs attention (the education of AIDS awareness in South Africa), it is probably related to your *vision*.

▼ **Discipline You** – Your *vision* will tell you what is important and what you need to give preference to. It will help you to maintain a healthy lifestyle by eating the right things and maintain a steady exercise regiment because you cannot afford to get sick. It will discipline how you spend your money whereas you will become conscious of the purchases you make. It will prioritize how you spend your time. *Vision* will tell you what to do and who to do it with, how to spend time and what to stay away from.

▼ **Set you Free from People Worship or Comparing Yourself to Others** – Your purpose tracks you for what you were born to do and no one else can do it like you can. No longer will you envy others or become jealous of others. You will learn what it means to rejoice when others rejoice because you know that if God has blessed other people in business, He will bless you as well. You will realize that you are just as important to God as those you place in high regard.

▼ **Determine your Friends, both Old and New** - The friends you used to have may not understand why you want to start your own company. They may not want to or be able to go with you on your journey when you decide to go into business (your journey to completing your purpose in life). Your attitude on life issues changes, as does your conversation. People who focus on the 'Eagle flying on Friday' or 'Living for the Weekend' somehow won't hold your interest. They are living for a paycheck and a party. You are living for a purpose to make an impact in the world around you. As you start your company you will meet other like-minded people in business that will not only become your friends but your confidants as well.

▼ ***Provide the Provisions*** – the money, resources, and people will follow your *vision*. Provision is hidden. It does not reveal itself until you need it. When you begin to take the first steps or walk towards the goals and plans of your *vision* (company) the provisions you need to succeed will manifest. Wherever there is a *vision*, God gives the provisions. He already has them prepared for you; all you need to do is ask for them. Wherever you see need, God will supply.

The reason you have these thoughts (*visions*) is because God gave them to you and He expects you to do something with them. That is what makes them original, God would not give you a copy of what is already in the earth unless it is to improve or perfect what is already here, thus making it something new again.

Here are three ***VISION RULES*** for realizing your *Vision*:

RULE #1 – *Write the Vision Down.*

▼ Regardless of what your thoughts, dreams, hopes, desires, goals or aspirations are, ***write them down***! No matter how short the thought, phrase, or sentence may be, jot it down on anything you can get your hands to write on. This is the beginning of your *vision*.

▼ Regardless of how crazy, senseless, or 'never been done before' thoughts and ideas you may have, ***write them down***. It will make sense later. (In Time)!

▼ Regardless of where you are or what you are doing, take the time to make a note of your thought. Record the date and time. If you can, record where you had the thought. Don't worry about what it looks like on paper.

▼ Keep a journal of your writings. Place your papers in a file jacket folder or a large envelope until you have time to transfer them into your journal. When you do, make sure you write it word for word. Better yet, paste or tape it to the paper in your journal. It's almost like making a scrapbook of your thoughts.

RULE #2 – *Find the Biblical Reference in the Bible for Your Vision.*

▼ There may be more than one scripture that speaks to your *vision*, it is okay to use both, just make sure they relate to each other.

▼ Measure your scripture reference verses with other translations to see if it verifies or confirms your *vision* for the company. Sometimes other translation meanings jump off the page at you and speak directly to you.

▼ The scripture reference will become the foundation for your *vision* so use the interpretation of them in your mission statement and *vision* statements.

▼ Make them a part of your daily meditation and confession of faith. Speak them to yourself until they become you. Think, eat and breathe your *vision*!

RULE #3– *Find a Business Mentor or Coach*

▼ Find someone who believes in what you want to do. Make sure he/she is a kingdom citizen and understand the principles of the Kingdom of God. In the beginning it is good to have only one because too many people will give you too many different opinions.

▼ This person should be able to direct you to learn more about the type of business you are pursuing and direct people and resources to you. He/She should be a person of influence and of high moral character. One that can have the power, ability and influence to bless your life.

▼ As your company grows I think it is a good idea to have more than one but no more than three. Each person should have expertise in the core competencies of the company and they need to understand what is important to you. These persons may become your board of advisers or directors of your company.

▼ They should get to know one another for your sake and meet with you on a regular basis. How often is up to you, however you should keep them abreast of what the status is of your business endeavors. (*See "Where To Go For More Information" in References for more information on Business Coaching.*)

Keep in mind that your business idea will need to be nurtured and cultivated and that is a process called *Time*. In that time you will have good days when it seems like your *vision* is about to manifest and not so good days when you think you might not have heard from God. This *time* is exactly what Dr. Cheryl Phillips told me the day after I had my first *vision* of starting my company. "Time will tell you if it is a true *vision* of God".

> *God puts a vision in your heart and soul that is a piece of eternity*
> *that He gave to deliver in TIME.*
> *What's in your heart is in His heart.*
> *That is a piece of his eternity in your TIME.*
> *This is what we call Deep calling unto Deep.*
> **Dr. Myles Munroe**

During your time of process (the nurturing of your business idea) don't forget to give God your praise and worship Him in true holiness for He is worthy of it all. It is because of God that we live, move and have our being. It is God who gives you ***purpose and vision: the perfect tag team*** for your company.

> *Purpose provides Your VISION.*
> *It gives precision to your life.*
> *The only things that should master you*
> *are the things that pertain to Your Vision.*
> **Carla A. Nelson**

BIBLICAL REFERENCE:

I will stand at my watch and station myself on the ramparts, I will look to see what he will say to me, and what answer I am to give to this complaint. Then the Lord's answer "Write down the revelation and make it plain on tablets so that a herald may run with it. For the revelation awaits an appointed time; it speaks of the end and will not prove false. Though it linger, wait for it; it will certainly come and will not delay".

Habakkuk 2:1-3 The Message

Blessed are the people who know the passwords of praise who shout on parade in the bright presence of God. Delighted, they dance all day long; they know who you are, what you do-they can't keep it quiet! Your vibrant beauty has gotten inside us - you've been so good to us! We're walking on air! All we are and have we owe to God, Holy God of Israel, our King! A long time ago your spoke in a vision, you spoke to your faithful beloved; I've crowned a hero, I chose the best I could find.

Psalm 89:15-19 The Message

VISION QUESTIONS:

1. Is the *vision* for your company a Natural Desire? Which area does your *vision* service a need to?

Economically _____   Educationally _____   Family _____
Medically _____   Socially _____
Spiritually _____

Explain:

2. Is the *vision* for your company a product or service to help others to do what they do better? Does it solve problems or fill a void of service that improves the life of others?

3. Is it something that is on your mind all the time? If money were not a factor (independently wealthy) would you do it for free?

4. Does the *vision* for your company inspire you? Does it motivate you when you get up in the morning or does it keep you up at night? How passionate are you about your idea? Do new thoughts and ideas go through your mind frequently?

5. Do you find yourself talking about your vision to others most of the time? If so, to whom do you discuss your vision idea with?

6. Does the *vision* for your company line up with God's word? Is it the RIGHT thing to do in your life or just a good thing for you?

7. Have you missed your opportunity (season) to make the *vision* for your company a reality or are you too early? Are you in God's time or yours?

SPIRITUAL PRINCIPLE #1
Purpose & Vision: The Perfect Tag Team (You can't have one without the other)

> *You are not saved to go to heaven.*
> *You are saved to finish an assignment given by God.*
>
> Dr. Myles Munroe

GOALS

BIBLICAL REFERENCE:
Seek ye the Lord while he may be found, call upon him while he is near: Let the wicked forsake his way, and the unrighteous man his thoughts: and let him return unto the Lord, and he will have mercy upon him; and to our God, for he will abundantly pardon. For my thoughts are not your thoughts, neither are your ways my ways, saith the Lord. For as the heavens are higher than the earth, so are my ways higher than your ways and my thoughts than your thoughts. For as the rain cometh down, and the snow from heaven, and returneth not thither, but watereth the earth, and maketh it bring forth bud that it may give seed to the sower and bread to the eater: So shall my word be that goeth forth out of my mouth: it shall not return unto me void, but it shall accomplished that which I please, and it shall prosper in the thing whereth I sent it.

> *Isaiah 55:6-11 KJV*

As I stated in Purpose, God does not play nine-inning games, He is not a quitter, He just plays until He wins. God is determined to get His Will accomplished in the earth. If one man or woman will not fulfill the purpose and vision for their life, God will wait for the next generation. Remember that God's time is eternal; it has no end. Since the word *goal* is not listed in the King James Version of the Bible, we must look for the right synonym to describe it **ACCOMPLISH** is the most appropriate word and can be found in the Bible.

Written goals help you determine the priorities for your company. As you begin to define the purpose and vision for your business idea, you will only want to do what is necessary to complete your assignment; you will become narrow-minded and determined to complete your assignment. Simply put *goals* are the on-going pursuit of a worthwhile desired objective until it is accomplished. *Goals* keep you focused on the end result no matter what the cost because you know you have heard from God. Paul said it best in the book of Philippians:

Brethren, I count not myself to have apprehended: but this one thing I do, forgetting those things which are behind, and reaching forth unto those things which are before, I press toward the mark for the prize of the high calling of God in Christ Jesus.
Philippians 3:13-14 KJV

I'm not saying that I have this all together, that I have it made. But I am well on my way, reaching out for Christ, who has so wondrously reached out for me. Friends, don't get me wrong; by no means do I count myself an expert in all of this, but I've got my eye on the goal, where God is beckoning us onward—to Jesus. I am off and running, and I'm not turning back.
Philippians 3:13-14 The Message

Clear written and well-defined *goals* are a vital process to identify what you must do and how you are to complete the vision for your company. The purpose of a *goal* is to set markers to accomplish a given task or assignment, no matter how great or how long. A *goal* is only complete once it is finished. Paul's life was one of great accomplishments. God used him to accomplish His purpose, to have the kingdom of God preached in every nation. Paul's teaching (letters to the churches) make up more than two-thirds of the New Testament, which is read throughout the world today. We will briefly look at the life of Paul to see how he was able to stay on course to complete his purpose in life by completing his *goal*. Paul states in 2 Timothy 4:7, that he had fought a good fight, finished his course, and kept the faith. I wonder how many of us are willing to go through the trials and tribulations of completing our purpose in life as Paul did for the sake of preaching the kingdom of God and the salvation of Jesus Christ. I wonder how many of us can say that at the end of our life we have fought a good fight, finished our course, and kept the faith to fulfill the purpose and vision for our life.

Paul was an educated and scholarly man with a zeal for the execution of the Hebrew law. Born a Roman citizen with a Jewish heritage of the tribe of Benjamin, both his heritage and education were vital to the knowledge of the Jewish law. His education gave him the knowledge, ability and influence to teach the salvation message of Jesus Christ and the Kingdom of God to the Jews. Acts 19:8, states that Paul spoke boldly in the synagogue for a space of three months, disputing and persuading the things concerning the kingdom of God. Somebody was listening, debating and receiving Paul's message! Even though Paul states in Philippians 3:5-11, he would consider all his education *loss* or *dung* that he may win Christ, it was his education and Roman citizenship that allowed him to proclaim Christ and His salvation to the Gentile world.

Paul's life is an excellent example of how God used his past experiences to make a difference in his future. In Philippians 3:4-6, Paul testifies to his birthright, education and zeal for doing right by way of the Hebrew law. As with us, Paul's habits did not change when he began teaching the principles of the Kingdom of God. He taught with the same zeal and tenacity as he did when he was a Pharisee.

Paul had a *goal* – to go to Rome and preach the kingdom of God and Jesus Christ. In Acts 19:21, it states that Paul had just completed preaching and starting churches in Ephesus. While traveling through Macedonia and Achaia on his way to Jerusalem, he purposed in his spirit to see (preach in) Rome. The Holy Spirit also witnessed to him that once in Jerusalem he would suffer bonds and afflictions. He even received a prophetic word from Agabus in Acts 21:10-14, but that still did not deter him from his *goal*.

As you read the travels of Paul in Acts 21-28, you will learn how he was falsely accused by the Jews and thrown in jail for two years. While there, Paul had a vision from the Lord - to bear witness of Him in Rome (Acts 23:11). Finally he was sent to Rome for his trial (and fulfill his *goal* of preaching in Rome), but he had to endure a storm that broke the ship he was on and once in Rome, wait another two years before he could appeal his case before Caesar. Regardless of Paul's physical condition, the environment in which he lived (in prison or handcuffed to a soldier), he never lost sight of his *goal*.

Paul accomplished his purpose in life, which was to go to Rome to *preach the kingdom of God and teach those things which concern the Lord Jesus Christ* to the Gentiles. His *goal* was to preach Jesus in Rome. We define *Goal* as *an aim; to set a boundary or limit; the terminal point of a race; the end toward which effort is directed; or the score resulting from such an act.*

Paul set boundaries and limits around his missionary journeys through the prompting of Holy Spirit. His aim was to get to Rome and all of his efforts were directed towards that end. Most importantly, Paul scored big time for Jesus by converting many Jews and Gentiles to live a life for Christ along his journey to Rome. We should also look at the word *Accomplish* since that is what we find in the Bible. *Accomplish* is defined as *to fill up; to complete or carry to completion; to bring to a successful conclusion; to attain to – a measure of time or distance; to cover; to equip thoroughly; or considered perfect.*

Paul brought his *goal* to a successful conclusion, being able to preach and teach in Rome. He was thoroughly equipped to do so being a Roman citizen, an educated man and a Pharisee. In addition, most of all, he carried out his purpose to completion, which is why he was able to say *I have finished my course.*

Goals should be clear, tangible, unique to your business market and measurable. They are comprised of objectives, tasks and assignments.

▼ *Objectives* – A strategic positioning to be attained or purpose to be achieved.

▼ *Tasks* – single elements that require action, when completed achieves the objective.

▼ *Assignments* – a specific task or amount of work assigned or undertaken as if assigned by authority.

Goals identify how you will fulfill your business idea (your vision). They give life to your purpose because they are the steps to fulfill your vision; the steps to *accomplish* your purpose for your company. *Goals* answer the *'who, what, when, where, why, and how questions'*:

▼ **Who you are going to do business with** – identify your customer profile

▼ **What type of company you will establish** – identify the Legal Structure of your company. *(See References for Legal Forms of Business Entities)*.

▼ **When you are to start your company** – identify a starting date to work full time in your company by setting a timeline and making realistic plans to reach your *goal*.

▼ **Where you are to do business** – identify the location (geographically and type of office structure) of your company. *(See Steps To Obtaining Office Space in Spiritual Principle #7)*.

▼ **Why you are to do business** – identify the products and services of your company and how they satisfy an unmet need in the earth. Another term for products and services is called *Profit Centers or Income Streams*.

▼ **How you are to conduct business** – identify the income streams of your company or how the products and services will make money.

Goals should not be stringent but they should be strategic and continuous because the completion of one *goal* is the beginning or process of a new *goal*. Continuous *goals* will keep you and your company from becoming stagnated! Well-established *goals* are:

▼ **Identifiers** – The things that are important to your purpose. You need to set *goals* for your personal life first, then for the life of your company. Your purpose will establish your personal *goals*, which become the foundation for your life – your fuel or reason for living. Purpose will solidify your vision, thus identifying the *goals* you are to set for your company.

▼ *Written* – Each *goal* must be in writing. They should have a start and completion date (or period of time) with a specific task or objective. These written *goals* will become a part of your planning process. They will determine how best you can *accomplish* them.

▼ *Motivators* – there will be times (seasons) when the company becomes difficult to maintain or the reasons why certain things are happening will seem illogical. Realize these moments are growing pains. Each written *goal* should serve to motivate you to keep striving to accomplish your dream (vision for the company).

▼ *Milestones* – set clear and reasonable markers for the growth and success of the business idea. Celebrate along the way as you complete each one, no matter how small! As they are completed, the objectives, tasks and assignments you wrote down that turn into milestones or *accomplishments*. When you look back and see how far you have come, you will be surprised as to how far you have traveled.

> *Good goals encourage the development of a good plan*
> **Dr. Myles Munroe**

As you set the *goals* for your business idea, there will be many things you can get involved in or include into the plan of your company that seem to be a good idea but are not right for the company. People will want you to incorporate their product or service into your business idea because they say it will complement the services you provide. Actually this is a way they make money off your sweat and labor. While you are promoting your company you are not only selling your product or service, but theirs as well. These people will reap the benefits of you promoting their goods to your prospective clients.

For instance, my company name has "Network" in it and our foundation is built on the *'networks'* or alliances we establish with other people, businesses and organizations. People who are in multi-level marketing organizations see how many people we are connected to and want to latch on to our contacts and our good name for their own financial gain. They tell us... *'You don't have to do any work, just sign up as a manager (representative, agent, WHATEVER) and we will do all the work. All you have to do is sign up, give us (anywhere from $49.99 to $495.00 or more), give us access to your contacts, sit back and collect a check each month. In no time at all you should be receiving a six-figure monthly income!'* The only person that gets the six-figure income is them at your expense. The time and effort you put into selling it to your clients!

Now how does that sound to you? God gives you this original idea to start a company that will help others and part of the reward for doing so is to live in the abundance. Why would you hand over your rewards (fruits of your labor) to someone else? I consider this unwise, foolish, and a downright sin. This would be transferring the wealth of the righteous (minded) into the hand of the wicked (minded). To do so is not keeping with your priorities; it does not push you forward to the place you want to be, and it definitely keeps you off track. I am not against the products or services found in multi-level marketing systems, however, I am against the methods they use to get people to join the organization.

Goals are the glue that binds together your purpose and vision for your company. They help you keep your purpose and vision in focus on a daily basis. Dr. Munroe describes *Goals* as *steps toward the desired end you set; creates, establishes and maintains your priorities; it determines who your companions are or will be; they dictate the choices you make in life; clear markers that will guide you towards your vision. They keep you tracked or focused; determines how you handle problems and distractions; they are the benefits of a vision; and they push you forward to the place you want to be.*

Lastly, do not add a service or product for the sake of increasing your revenues. If the service or product does not directly relate to your core competencies, don't include it. Remember, *goals* are clear marks that guide you towards your vision and will determine how you handle distractions. If you must, re-read your *goals* to determine if you are to include a new product or service. To do so and then realize you lost more money than you thought you would make, is a waste of your time, God's time and His resources, and God is not a wasteful God!

Goals provide the destination to your destiny (purpose) and
Each destiny has a route.
Each route contains markers (goals) to
Guide you along the way towards your expected end (vision).
Make sure your markers are set straight to accomplish the goals
for your company!

Dr. Myles Munroe & Carla A. Nelson

BIBLICAL REFERENCE:

Seek God while he's here to be found, pray to him while he's close at hand. Let the wicked abandon their way of life and the evil their way of thinking. Let them come back to God, who is merciful, come back to our God who is lavish with forgiveness. I don't think the way you think. The way you work isn't the way I work. God's Decree. For as the sky soars high above the earth, so the way I work surpasses the way you work, and the way I think is beyond the way you think. Just as rain and snow descend from the skies and don't go back until they've watered the earth, doing their work of making things grow and blossom, producing seed for farmers and food for the hungry, so will the words that come out of my mouth not come back empty-handed.

Isaiah 55:6-11 The Message

GOAL QUESTIONS:

1. Do you keep a journal specifically for your business idea (vision)? Record the date and time of each new thought as well as the date and time that thought (idea) became a reality? (Milestones).

2. What are the tasks you need to accomplish in a certain period of time? Write them down with specific timelines. (Be realistic).

3. Do your goals indicate Who your customers are, WHAT type of company you want to start, WHEN you plan to start working full time in the company, WHERE you want the company to be located, WHY the company must exist, and HOW you intend to make money?

4. What resources or provisions (people and materials) will you need to accomplish your goals? Who are the people, organizations, equipment and supplies you will need to accomplish your goals? Write them down with each task listed above.

5. Do your goals (objectives, task, and assignments) end with a new one to be accomplished?

SPIRITUAL PRINCIPLE #1
Purpose & Vision: The Perfect Tag Team (You can't have one without the other)

A Mission guides your decisions and determines your strategy for success!
Shelly Gross-Wade

MISSION AND VISION STATEMENTS

BIBLICAL REFERENCE:
"I must preach the kingdom of God to other cities also: for therefore am I sent".

Luke 4:43 KJV

When you begin a company (business, organization, church or ministry), the first thing you must do is declare what your company is suppose to do. The *Mission Statement* should express why the company exists. In Matthew 4:17, the first public statement of Jesus became His purpose. *"Repent for the kingdom of heaven is at hand"* (or *has arrived on earth*). In Luke 4:18-19 Jesus gives us His Mission and Vision Statement: *"The Spirit of the Lord is upon me, because he hath anointed me to preach the gospel to the poor; he hath sent me to heal the brokenhearted, to preach deliverance to the captives, and recovering of sight to the blind, to set at liberty them that are bruised, to preach the acceptable year of the Lord".* The only reason Jesus came to the earth was to preach the Kingdom of God. The purpose for Jesus' life was clearly stated, His mission and vision was clearly defined; His goals were concrete and He completed His mission before He left the earth.

The *Mission Statement* for your company should indicate what it is to accomplish. It is a concise statement of the overall purpose and direction of the company. It speaks to the quality and value of the assignment or service to be performed or the work to be produced. *Mission Statements* are also referred to as a *Tribute*, something given or contributed voluntarily as due or deserved. The statement should speak to respect, gratitude or affection of your customers and clients, and speaks to the worth, virtue and effectiveness of the company.

Mission is defined as *the act or an instance of sending; an assignment to or work in a field of missionary enterprise; a body of persons sent to perform a service or carry on an activity; a group sent to a foreign country to conduct diplomatic or political negotiations; a team of specialists or cultural leaders sent to a foreign country; a specific task with which a person or group is charged; or a Calling or Vocation.*

Your Mission Statement should answer these questions:

> *1. Who is your customer or what is your market?*
> *2. What is your product or service?*
> *3. What is your special competency, strength, or uniqueness?*

Most business books state that your company mission should only be one sentence, however, the *Mission Statement* can consist of several sentences, but should be only one paragraph long.

Write your Mission Statement:

The *Vision Statement* for your company should indicate what is the passion for your company. What is it that drives you to do what you do? It indicates the original intent of the company; what the company is to accomplish. It is that unique thought that keeps you awake at night. The *Vision Statement* is your sustainer, especially through the rough times. If you need to, go back to the section on vision to read what vision is in order to write your vision statement.

Unlike the mission for the company which is usually one sentence, the vision for your company may be quite lengthy. The clearer you see what it is you are purposed to do the larger your vision. The *Vision Statement* will consist of several sentences and possibly more than one paragraph but no more than two.

Write your Vision Statement:

BIBLICAL REFERENCE:
"Don't you realize that there are other villages where I have to tell the Message of God's kingdom, that this is the work God sent me to do"?
Luke 4:43 The Message

NOTES

SPIRITUAL PRINCIPLE #2
Faith & Prayer: Building A Firm Foundation (A deep foundation will endure any storm)

Faith is the material substance by which I bring
My vision (for the company)
To pass (become a reality).

Dr. Myles Munroe

FAITH

BIBLICAL REFERENCE:
...Therefore I say unto you, Take no thought for your life, what ye shall eat; neither for the body, what ye shall put on. The life is more than meat, and the body is more than raiment. Consider the ravens: for they neither sow nor reap; which neither have storehouse nor barn; and God feedeth them: how much more are ye better than the fowls? And which of you with taking thought can add to his stature one cubit? If ye then be not able to do that thing which is least, why take ye thought for the rest? Consider the lilies how they grow: they toil not, they spin not; and yet I say unto you, that Solomon in all his glory was not arrayed like one of these. If then God so clothe the grass, which is to day in the field, and to morrow is cast into the oven; how much more will he clothe you, O ye of little faith? And seek not ye what ye shall eat, or what ye shall drink, neither be ye of doubtful mind. For all these things do the nations of the world seek after: and your Father knoweth that ye have need of these things. But rather seek ye the kingdom of God; and all these things shall be added unto you.

Luke 12:22-31 KJV

To be faithful is a time-tested attribute. Your *faith* has to be consistent and proven. You have to be found faithful in whatever you do. You must be faithful to your business idea even when circumstances of it becoming a reality look UGLY. It is at this time when you must increase your level of *faith* in God. Just because you have this great idea or vision from God to go into business does not mean that everything will be perfect along the way. The infancy stage of the business idea is when the enemy tries to kill your vision. It is during these times you will discover if you are truly faithful to the vision that God gave you.

Faith is to believe or trust in God, to abide in Him. It is an allegiance to duty or a person; loyalty; fidelity to one's promises; the belief, trust in, and loyalty to God; a firm belief in something for which there is no proof; the complete confidence; or something that is believed especially with strong conviction, especially a system of religious beliefs. It is during the infancy stage that keeping company with God is vital to the development of your business idea.

To be *Faithful is to be full of faith; steadfast in affection or allegiance; loyal or conscientious. To be firm in adherence to promises or in observance of duty; given with strong assurance. It is binding, or true to the facts or to an original. Faithfulness is to be full of faith as a church member in full communion and good standing. A loyal follower or member of a party or organization.*

Everything in your company has to be **made, managed** and **multiplied**. This pertains to your service or product, customers and clients, employees, and most of all the money!
Most people are good at the making and the multiplication, but not at the management. Notice that word is in the middle of the **MAKE** and the **MULTIPLY**. If you cannot **MANAGE** properly, there will be nothing to **MULTIPLY** and to manage properly is what you need to do in order to have a successful company and to provide for the kingdom of God.

To manage properly you must have a certain degree of skill and experience with the products or services your company will provide. To manage properly you will have to make many adjustments in order to succeed in accomplishing the goals you set for the company. Managing your company is like nurturing your newborn baby, and in many ways your business idea is like giving birth to a baby called _____ (insert the name of your business idea or company name).

I am sure you are wondering what does your company have to do with providing for the kingdom of God. I am glad you asked! Providing for the kingdom of God includes your church by giving tithes and offering from your company account; your employees by ensuring there is sufficient money to provide a steady payroll; and the business community by adding to the economic base in your city. Mismanagement comes from not understanding how to handle situations in your company. The things that are mismanaged will lead to slack. The things that are left to slack will lead to lack, and lack will show up in your revenue stream. When you realize you do not understand how to manage a particular part of your business operations or how to handle an employee or customer situation, you must get wisdom! That is the reason why you have a mentor or a business coach. Use them! (*We covered this in* **Vision Rules** *in Spiritual Principle #1 and we will discuss this in more detail in Spiritual Principle #7 in the section called* **The Red Team***).*

Not slothful in business, fervent in spirit; serving the Lord; Rejoicing in hope; patient in tribulation; continuing instant in prayer; Distributing to the necessity of saints; given to hospitality.

Romans 12:11-13 KJV

Don't burn out; keep yourselves fueled up and aflame. Be alert servants of the Master, cheerfully expectant. Don't quit in hard times; pray all the harder. Help needy Christians; be inventive in hospitality.

Romans 12:11-13 The Message

The results I receive in my company are directly related to the degree of faith I possess and exercise.
The measure of faith I have is not the measure of faith I should maintain.
My faith should increase as I mature.

Carla A. Nelson

The Four Powerful P's of Faith

Your *faith* makes way for **Provision, Perfection, Promotion** and **Protection** from God. Since the vision for your business came from God, He is required to make sure you receive the necessary **Provisions** to maintain and succeed in business. Even when you think you are about to go under, you will not suffer lack. Remember your part is to confess the word of God daily as you begin your day. The things you need to make your company prosperous will be given to you as you move forward with your business idea. Without movement (constantly doing something to improve the company) there will be no need for God to **Provide** for it.

(O Lord) ...give unto Solomon my son (put your name here) a perfect heart, to keep thy commandments, thy testimonies, and thy statutes, and to do all these things, and to build the palace (your business), for the which I have made provision.
1 Chronicles 29:19 KJV

As you become more experienced in your business (or even in your career), you will begin to see the **Perfection** of God in you and the things in your company. There will be times when you wonder why you had to go through a bad or unpleasant experience or how could you have been so naïve in a certain situation. God will always **Perfect** you first to be the person He needs you to be in business before He increases the business operations (being responsible) and revenues (profits).

Though I walk in the midst of trouble, thou wilt revive me: thou shalt stretch forth thine hand against the wrath of mine enemies, and thy right hand shall save me. The Lord will perfect that which concerneth me; thy mercy, O Lord, endureth for ever: forsake not the works of thine own hands.
Psalm 138:7-8 KJV

Your **Promotion** will come in the form of better business relation-ships, you will be known throughout the community, which is one way to become a person of influence. You will receive large or long-term business contracts because you are the expert. You will be **Promoted** because you know what you are doing and you can be trusted. Others will speak of your good works, which is how you obtain a good reputation.

Lift not up your horn on high: speak not with a stiff neck. For promotion cometh neither from the east, nor from the west, nor from the south. But God is the judge: he putteth down one, and setteth up another.
Psalm 75:5-6 KJV

Most of all the **Protection** of God is important to you and your company. No matter what others might say about you and your business idea, as long as you are obedient to God's word in your life and the life of your company, He will always **Protect** you from the hand of the enemy. This enemy can take the form of naysayers, people trying to ruin your reputation, or those who want to steal your business idea.

O love the Lord, all his saints: for the Lord preserveth the faithful, and plentifully rewardeth the proud doer. Be of good courage, and he shall strengthen your heart, all ye that hope in the Lord.

Psalm 31:23KJV

It takes *faith* to pursue your business idea when no one believes in you or your dream. A key element to make sure your business idea is from God is to take it to Him in prayer. You must have *faith* in God or the God kind of *faith* if you expect your business idea to manifest.

Therefore I say unto you, What things soever ye desire, when ye pray, believe that ye receive them, and ye shall have them.

Mark 11:24 KJV

This verse is considered the *Prayer of Faith. Faith* is required to produce the written promises God has for you according to His word. This verse tells us that you have to believe what you pray for when you are actually saying the prayer. Don't wait on the manifestation of your prayer; believe that it has come when you are praying. What you have need of, is already in the spiritual realm, you are just making a demand to receive what is already yours!

You when you are in *faith*, you must confess the word of God on a daily basis and believe it in your heart that what you confess will manifest. As a result you will receive:

▼ *The Wisdom of God*
▼ *A Plan of God*
▼ *The Favor of God*
▼ *Expect the Miraculous to happen*
▼ *Have the Strength to Endure until change comes*

Dr. Ira V. Hilliard

Now the just shall live by faith; but if any man draw back, my soul shall have no pleasure in him.

Hebrews 10:38 KJV

Faith is NOW. *Faith* is progressive. It is always in a positive position. That is why it is so important to remain positive during the struggles and valleys that you go through in your business and in life. Active *faith* is how you keep your angels active as they work on your behalf (minister) for you. *Faith* is not about feelings and emotions. There is no sight in *faith*. You cannot rely on your five senses to determine if you are in *faith* or not. You must remain in constant faith by living a godly lifestyle and keeping your commitment to what you set out to do in your company. Remain committed to the things God reveals to you in His vision for your life.

My first real test of *faith* for my business (to actualize the manifestation) came on Sunday, June 9, 1996. Minister and Motivational Speaker, Alphonso (Al) Way was the keynote speaker at our church's Graduation Ceremony for those who had completed any level of education, from Kindergarten to Ph.D. During his charge to the students, he spoke from Psalms 126 *I'm Going To The Next Level*. His words spoke directly to ME because I was moving towards the next level in my business by looking for office space. Pastor Phillips mentioned him to me in a previous conversation indicating we might be able to work together on some projects since we had some of the same business skills in common.

Pastor Phillips and I were not having much success in finding an office space that I could afford and I began to wonder if this was the right move; I began to question if I had really heard from God. I got the opportunity to speak to Minister Way after the service and asked him if I could call upon him for consultation. He was more than willing to assist me in any way he could.

On June 20, 1996 at 10:00 a.m., I spoke to Minister Way regarding my success in finding office space for my business. This is what he said to me:

▼ *Faith is my response to obedience to do God's word—His Logos word*
▼ *Faith is a leap into the light*
▼ *Faith is what I need to take the power out of disappointment*
▼ *Faith is how I glorify God regardless and He will manifest the best for me*
▼ *Faith is how I learn to know God's voice*

Things I needed to do:

1. *Negotiation – the price for the Office Space*
2. *Prepare a Capability Statement - one sheet*
3. *Get on his calendar to talk again*

In closing, Minister Way said the office space I found would not be the office space I would move into; God had something else in mind for me. I thought – this man does not know how hard it was to find this one! Is he crazy or is **wisdom** speaking?

Around 3:00 p.m. I received a call from my real estate broker. He said the plans and financial statements I gave to the leasing manager for the office space I saw would not support the amount of work that needed to be done to move into it. However, the leasing manager had another space that I might be interested in that was less money but more square footage. 'How could that be?' I thought, but I was surely interested in seeing the space.

I remember praying to God while driving on the 495 Beltway that I would receive the favor of man for this office space. God knew how much money I had and the kind of office space I truly desired. God knew the **plan** I had for my business and what it was suppose to accomplish. All I needed was God to bless me in this situation and hope it was not a fluke.

I met the leasing manager, Bob Depew at his office around 4:00 p.m. We talked briefly about my business concept. He was very interested and suggested I become a member of the Prince George's Chamber of Commerce (which I joined and years later became a member of the Board of Directors). Bob showed me the layout of the office space. It was 500 square feet larger and $10.00 a square foot cheaper than the first place we (Pastor and I) saw. Bob explained why it was less expensive and that the place had not been used in over 18 months. It needed some work but I was ready and willing to take it on. At that point I realized that I had received the **favor** of God. When I got in my car the first thing I said was "Thank you God for your Grace."

After the meeting with Bob Depew I called Minister Way and told him what happened. I was crying because I was so happy and thanked him for his prophetic word. He told me that the number 5 was representative of the word *Grace* and it was approximately five hours from the time we had the conversation that morning to the time I saw the office space! Needless to say the **miraculous** had happened and I was so overwhelmed with the way God showed off in my life.

On Saturday, June 29, 1996, around 11:00 p.m. after much discussion and review with Pastor Phillips and prayer, I finally signed the office lease papers. I wanted it to be exactly four years from the day I came up with the name for my business Visionary Network Consultants. God gave me the **strength to endure** in pursuing my business idea/vision of starting a business with no prior business experience than becoming an independent consultant that afforded me the money to obtain office space.

On Sunday, July 7, 1996, I realized that this office space must be of God because it was bigger than me. As much as I see in my mind's eye of how I want it to look, yet I can't see how I can afford it. At the same time I kept going forward, I felt like I was being pushed to continue, my *faith* was being challenged and increased at the same time. I didn't see how I could pull it off. That's when I realized this is God's doing, not mine. This thing is bigger than me, which is all the more reason why I needed *faith* in God to pull it off. This was my **change**. This was my first **manifestation** in my business life.

Keep thy heart with all diligence; for out of it are the issues of life
Proverbs 4:23 KJV

Keep vigilant watch over your heart; that's where life starts.
Proverbs 4:23 The Message

Whatever idea (seed) I put in my heart (soil)
Will appear in my life (the manifested harvest).
Dr. Charles Phillips

During the process of starting your business, your *faith* in your business idea will always be determined by what you feed your spirit, and in what you see, say and hear. If you want the vision of your business to manifest, not only do you need to make sure God is in it, you must guard your idea from those who don't believe in you or those who wish to sabotage you and your idea.

   ▼ *What are You Listening to?*
   ▼ *Who are You Listening to?*
   ▼ *What are You Looking at?*
   ▼ *Who are You Looking at?*
   ▼ *What are You Talking about?*
   ▼ *Who are You Talking to?*

What is on your mouth most of the time when you are talking to someone?
That is what is in your heart in abundance.
Dr. Charles Phillips

Therefore you must remember that *faith* is also a spiritual weapon that we, the Saints of God, have at our disposal to head off the attacks from the enemy, be them real (other people) or imagined (your own negative thoughts). When you speak *faith*-filled words over your business idea and its circumstances, the angels respond to God's word and protect you from the enemy. This is vitally important to you while you are in *faith* for your change (business idea) to manifest. *(The ministering of Angels will be discussed in Spiritual Principle #5).*

BIBLICAL REFERENCE:

Don't fuss about what's on the table at mealtimes or if the clothes in your closet are in fashion. There is far more to your inner life than the food you put in your stomach, more to your outer appearance than the clothes you hang on your body. Look at the ravens, free and unfettered, not tied down to a job description, carefree in the care of God. And you count far more. Has anyone by fussing before the mirror ever gotten taller by so much as an inch? If fussing can't even do that, why fuss at all? Walk into the fields and look at the wildflowers. They don't fuss with their appearance – but have you ever seen color and design quite like it? The ten best-dressed men and women in the country look shabby alongside them. If God gives such attention to the wildflowers, most of them never even seen, don't you think he'll attend to you, take pride in you, do his best for you? What I'm trying to do here is get you to relax, not be so preoccupied with getting so you can respond to God's giving. People who don't know God and the way he works fuss over these things, but know both God and how he works. Steep yourself in God-reality, God –initiatives, God-provisions. You'll find all your everyday human concerns will be met. Don't be afraid of missing out. You're my dearest friends! The Father wants to give you the very kingdom itself.

Luke 12:22-31 The Message

FAITH QUESTIONS:

1. Can you be found faithful to your own business even when it seems like it is going to fail?

2. Can God count on you to be dependable over the long haul?

3. Can God rely on you to produce the gift and talent He put in you and to multiply it for the Kingdom of God?

4. Do others consider you to be loyal and trustworthy?

5. According to Mark 11:24, do you have the "*I believe that I have received*" kind of *faith* when you pray or do you have the "*I believe it when I see it*" kind of *faith*?

SPIRITUAL PRINCIPLE #2
Faith & Prayer: Building A Firm Foundation (A deep foundation will endure any storm)

Prayer gives the believer wisdom that surpasses the education,
pedigree or status of the world.
It allows God to intervene in your affairs and do things that defies
the logic of man.

Dr. Charles Phillips

PRAYER

BIBLICAL REFERENCE:
"For verily I say unto you, That whosoever shall say unto this mountain, Be thou removed, and be thou cast into the sea; and shall not doubt in his heart, but shall believe that those things which he saith shall come to pass; he shall have whatsoever he saith. Therefore I say unto you, What things soever ye desire, when ye pray, believe that ye receive them, and ye shall have them. And when ye stand praying, forgive, if ye have ought against any: that your Father also which is in heaven may forgive you your trespasses. But if ye do not forgive, neither will your Father which is in heaven forgive your trespasses".
Mark 11:23-26 KJV

The first thing you do when you wake up in the morning is PRAY. Your day should not start without it. Your feet should not even hit the floor without acknowledging God and thanking Him for granting you another day. Along with praying for a successful day and the safety of you and your family, you should also pray for your business. There is nothing wrong or selfish to pray for the prosperity (good success) of your business. Why else would God give you the vision for it? Thank Him for your business everyday and ask for the wisdom to see creative ideas and hear the best deals (opportunities) to bring increase to your business.

A whole book could be written on *prayer* but here are a few ways in which *prayer* can be used. *Prayer* is defined as *an address (as a petition) to God in a word or thought; a set order of words used in praying; an earnest request; the act or practice of praying to God; or something prayed for.* To be *Prayerful* is to be *devout, earnest or sincere.*

The first mention of *prayer* is in Genesis 4:25-26 *And to Seth, to him also there was born a son; and he called his name Enos: then began men to call upon the name of the LORD.* But it is Jeremiah 33:2-3 (the verse that most people call God's telephone number) that we see Jeremiah praying to God for an answer to his situation. *Thus saith the LORD the maker thereof, the LORD that formed it, to establish it; the LORD is his name; Call unto me, and I will answer thee, and show thee great and mighty things, which thou knowest not.*

Prayer is the foundation of life for the citizen of the kingdom of God. To have your business idea come to fruition, you must be an effective and responsive citizen in God's kingdom. It is important for you to be near to God when He speaks. *Prayer* is the communication method God uses to get your answers.

▼ *Prayer is Active* – it requires your participation. You must give voice to your *prayers* so that God and you can hear them. The mind will begin to believe what you say when you pray and begin to prepare to receive (conception) what you *prayed* for. It puts you in a state of readiness. Be mindful of how you talk and the words you use. Your words are the seeds and your heart is the soil. What you say (your confessions) will be planted in your heart therefore, what you sow will eventually grow, be it positive or negative.

And this is the confidence that we have in him, that, if we ask any thing according to his will, he heareth us: And if we know that he hear us, whatsoever we ask, we know that we have the petitions that we desired of him.
1 John 5:14-15 KJV

And how bold and free we then become in his presence, freely asking according to his will sure that he's listening. And if we're confident that he's listening, we know that what we've asked for is as good as ours.
1 John 5:14-15 The Message

▼ *Prayer is a Spiritual Weapon* - it will cover and provide a hedge of protection around you and your company as you go out into the world conducting your business affairs. Psalm 91 is an excellent *prayer* to say every morning. The more you recite it the more you will find yourself adding your specific requests within each verse of this Psalm. Personalize it for yourself and see how God answers your *prayer* based on each one of the verses.

I remember verbalizing this Psalm on July 8, 1998 while getting ready for work in Philadelphia where my consulting assignment was (I live in Maryland and it is a two hour commute by car each way). There was a terrible rainstorm and I thought about turning around several times as I reached Baltimore. Against my better judgment (of not wanting to lose a day's pay and be looked upon as a wimp by my peers) I continued on.

I continued to pray for safety and thanked God I was not one of the many people whose car was stranded on the side of the road. As I approached my exit towards Wayne PA, I hydroplaned into the back of a SUV. No damage was done to the SUV or the driver, but my car was completely totaled and my airbag was deployed, however I did not have a single scratch or bruise.

The State Trooper looked at my car and was amazed that I was not hurt. I was upset and I asked God why did He let this happen? I prayed Psalm 91 and that I would not have any accidents. God's reply to me as plain as someone speaking to me. He said "You prayed that the angels would have charge over you and your foot would not be dashed against a stone. Look at your feet; are they hurt? Look at your body; is it broken? You can get another car but you cannot get another body". I immediately stopped my complaining attitude, gave God praise all day long, and told everyone I could tell that God kept me. What makes this story more compelling is that my father died in a car accident by losing control of his car and ran it front first into a tree. The tree is still standing there today with some of its bark missing but my father did not survive the injuries to his internal organs. But for the grace of God this could have been my end on this day.

For he shall give his angels charge over thee, to keep thee in all thy ways. They shall bear thee up in their hands, lest thou dash thy foot against a stone.

Psalm 91:11-12 KJV

He ordered his angels to guard you wherever you go. If you stumble, they'll catch you; their job is to keep you from falling.

Psalm 91:11-12 The Message

▼ *Prayer takes panic out of a negative situation* – it will grant you favor with man when your financial picture indicates you cannot afford the office space, equipment, supplies, or printing materials that you need to start your business. They will decide to sell it to you at a lower cost or give it to you because they want your business to succeed (this is another form of investment or planting seed). Remember, God is the one who qualifies you!

O Lord, I beseech thee, let now thine ear be attentive to the prayer of thy servant, and to the prayer of thy servants, who desire to fear thy name: and prosper, I pray thee, thy servant this day, and grant him mercy in the sight of this man. For I was the king's cupbearer.

Nehemiah 1:11 KJV

O Master, listen to me, listen to your servant's prayer – and yes, to all your servants who delight in honoring you – and make me successful today so that I get what I want from the king. I was cupbearer to the king.

Nehemiah 1:11 The Message

▼ *Prayer is a stress reliever* – it will help you to calm down during and after a rough day. It will help you to regain your inner balance when everything around you is out of balance. It is important to live a balanced lifestyle. *Prayer* equals power in the life of a citizen of the kingdom of God. I have come to learn that the short prayer *"peace be still"* is truly powerful and really does work!

Rejoice in the Lord alway: and again I say, Rejoice. Let your moderation be known unto all men. The Lord is at hand. Be careful for nothing; but in every thing by prayer and supplication with thanksgiving let your requests be made known unto God. And the peace of God, which passeth all understanding, shall keep your hearts and minds through Christ Jesus.

Philippians 4:4-7 KJV

Celebrate God all day, every day. I mean, revel in him! Make it as clear as you can to all you meet that you're on their side, working with them. Help them see that the Master is about to arrive. He could show up at any minute! Don't fret or worry. Instead of worrying, pray. Let petitions and praises shape your worries into prayers, letting God know your concerns. Before you know it, a sense of God's wholeness, everything coming together for good, will come and settle you down. It's wonderful what happens when Christ displaces worry at the center of your life.

Philippians 4:4-7 The Message

If you pray, don't worry. If you worry, don't pray! Sounds simple but it is not all that easy, especially during the times of anticipation to receive your answer or to resolve a serious problem you are facing. That is why Faith and *Prayer* go hand in hand to build your foundation. When you pray to ask God for something, believe (have the faith) that He has already given it to you. From then on you begin to daily thank Him for the answer until the answer or manifestation arrives. Remember that the duration between your *prayer* request (seed) and the evidence of your *prayer* (harvest) is called TIME. Use this duration of time to give God praise and thanksgiving for the success of your business idea, the answers to your questions, and the solutions to your problems.

Praise and worship, meditation, and reading scriptures can all be incorporated during your *prayer* time. It will usher in Holy Spirit, cause the devil to flee from you, and give you peace, joy and happiness. After your *prayer* time you will have a sound mind, a clean heart, and the wisdom of God to be creative and prosperous! What a way to start the day! Who needs *Kellogg's Special K or One a Day?* When you start your day with *prayer*, you can't help yourself from having a successful day!

Your *prayers* should be specific. Don't just ask God to bless you. As a believer in the kingdom of God you are already blessed with all spiritual blessings. You need to tell God exactly what it is you desire for your company. God already has it in a room with your name on it; He is just waiting on you to ask for your stuff! You should know what it is you desire because you wrote it down in your *Mission and Vision Statements as discussed in Spiritual Principle #1.*

When you pray, have the confidence that God hears you and will answer your *prayers* according to His Will and His word. Do not pray based on your feelings or your plans regarding the business no matter how bad it looks like in the natural. *Prayers* are not about your feelings and emotions. That is why God does not respond to your tears and frustration; He only responds to His word that you recite out of your mouth. *I should know. I have a mascara stain on a pillowcase I cried on for hours begging God to answer me some years ago when I did not know how I was going to get out of a situation. The very next day God answered my prayer in a mighty way and told me all that crying I did was a waste of time and energy. He already had the answer but I was too impatient to wait for it even though I recited His words! Needless to say I don't cry like that anymore!*

Not only does crying not move God, but neither does fasting. Fasting is for you to correct your flesh and move you into the right position so you can begin to *receive* from God. *Prayer* is when you give God the legal right to interfere in your affairs! There is a hierarchy in how you should pray to God.

1. **Be Quiet.** You should be in a place that is silent so that you will not be distracted by outside noises. *(See the section on Silent in Spiritual Principle #3).*
2. **Give Adoration.** God deserves the proper protocol, respect, and all the praise, worship and glory.
3. **Make Your Confessions.** Agree with God about what He says *about you* in His word, and what He will say *to you* during your *prayer* time.
4. **Give Thanks.** Now you are free to praise Him and hear from Him with a clean and righteous heart.
5. **Specify Your Petition and Request.** God cannot answer ambiguity. If you need to, read the written goals for your company to Him for what you desire.
6. **Plead Your Case.** Put God in remembrance of His word. Quote the scriptures to back up your *prayer* request.
7. **Believe.** Regardless of what it looks like, believe that you have received the answers to your *prayer*. Be consistent, everyday, all the time!

8. ***Give Thanks.*** Always close your *prayer* with thanksgiving to God for His answers and for the manifestation of your *prayer* request.

God is very technical so in order to get your *prayers* answered effectively you will need to do the following on a consistent basis:

▼ When you pray SAY. You have to speak in an audible voice so that you can be heard.
And it came to pass, that, as he was praying in a certain place, when he ceased, one of his disciples said unto him, Lord, teach us to pray, as John also taught his disciples. And he said unto them, "When ye pray, say, Our Father which art in heaven, Hallowed be thy name. Thy kingdom come. Thy will be done, as in heaven, so in earth"... Luke 11:1-2 KJV

▼ *Prayer* activates your faith by asking, seeking, and knocking for the things you have asked God for.
"Ask, and it shall be given you; seek, and ye shall find; knock, and it shall be opened unto you: For every one that asketh receiveth; and he that seeketh findeth; and to him that knocketh it shall be opened". Matthew 7:7-8 and Luke 11:9-10 KJV

▼ Believe that you have already received what you asked for during your *prayer* time. From that point on just thank God for the manifestation of your *prayer*.
"For verily I say unto you, That whosoever shall say unto this mountain, Be thou removed, and be thou cast into the sea; and shall not doubt in his heart, but shall believe that those things which he saith shall come to pass; he shall have whatsoever he saith. Therefore I say unto you, What things soever ye desire, when ye pray, believe that ye receive them, and ye shall have them". Mark 11:23-24 KJV

▼ You must be consistent and effective in *prayer*. Praying in the spirit will set you outside of the limitations of your life into the unlimited realm of God.
And these signs shall follow them that believe; In my name shall they cast out devils; they shall speak with new tongues. Mark 16:17 KJV

▼ Always pray and ask for what you desire in the name of Jesus Christ who is the Son of God for it is through Him your *prayer* is answered.

"And in that day ye shall ask me nothing. Verily, verily, I say unto you, Whatsoever ye shall ask the Father in my name, he will give it you. Hitherto have ye asked nothing in my name: ask, and ye shall receive, that your joy may be full". John 16:23-24 KJV

Thank you Father that you always hear my prayers.
I rest in the fact that there is no lack in my life or in the life of my company.
The devil has no plot or lot in this matter, (my business idea)
For this is not my battle (the success of my company), but the Lord's.
May I be found in the place call THERE!
I don't want to be found in the place called WHERE?

Carla A. Nelson

While we are on the subject of *prayer*, I must address the topic of *Praying in the Spirit* or *Speaking in Tongue*. It is a topic that has caused many arguments in various Christian church denominations. Some believe in it, others do not, and there are some that say it died out with the Apostles. Let me be clear on this subject. Speaking in an unknown tongue is real, effective and necessary for a citizen of the kingdom of God because it is the official language of the kingdom of God!

And when the day of Pentecost was fully come, they were all with one accord in one place. And suddenly there came a sound from heaven as of a rushing mighty wind, and it filled all the house where they were sitting. And there appeared unto them cloven tongues like as of fire, and it sat upon each of them. And they were all filled with the Holy Ghost, and began to speak with other tongues, as the Spirit gave them utterance.

Acts 2:1-5 KJV

Speaking in Tongues is what we call your *Prayer Language* and God's direct method of communication. Speaking in tongues cannot be interpreted or understood by satan or you! It is the language communicated between your spirit through Holy Spirit directly to God.

Follow after charity, and desire spiritual gifts, but rather that ye may prophesy. For he that speaketh in an unknown tongue speaketh not unto men, but unto God: for no man understandeth him; howbeit in the spirit he speaketh mysteries.

1 Corinthians 14:1-2 KJV

Although you may not understand with your mind what it is you are praying for, take comfort in knowing that your spirit man knows and will only ask of God what is best for you. You do have the ability and the right to ask God for the interpretation of your *prayer*, so before you stop praying, remember to ask God for the revelation knowledge of your prayer. He is faithful to honor that request as well.

Wherefore let him that speaketh in an unknown tongue pray that he may interpret. For if I pray in an unknown tongue, my spirit prayeth, but my understanding is unfruitful. What is it then? I will pray with the spirit, and I will pray with the understanding also: I will sing with the spirit, and I will sing with the understanding also.

1 Corinthians 14:13-15 KJV

Since satan cannot understand what your spirit is saying, he cannot stop what you (your spirit man) is requesting or saying to God. This frustrates him, therefore, he will use any tactic he can to get you to stop or never begin to speak in tongues. These tactics include arguments and dissension in the church. Some people will look at you strange or ask you why would you say something that does not make sense. The worst is to allow satan to influence your thoughts that it is a waste of your time and to speak in tongues is utter nonsense!

Praying in the spirit is the most effective spiritual weapon you have as a resource so USE IT! Be diligent in your *prayer* time. You should devote at least one hour a day, preferably in the morning as you start your day. As you grow in your *prayer* time with God, increase it to allow one-tenth of your day (2.4 hours). This does not have to be all at the same time, just make sure you get it in. God's communication vehicle is available 24/7/365!

BIBLICAL REFERENCE:
"Embrace this God-life. Really embrace it, and nothing will be too much for you, This mountain, for instance: Just say, 'Go jump in the lake"-no shuffling or shilly – shallying – and it is as good as done. That's why I urge you to pray for absolutely everything, ranging from small to large. Include everything as you embrace this God-life, and you'll get God's everything. And when you assume the posture of prayer, remember that it's not all asking. If you have anything against someone, forgive – only then will your heavenly Father be inclined to also wipe your slate clean of sins".

Mark 11:23-26 The Message

PRAYER QUESTIONS:

1. Do you pray with all of your heart and believe that you receive (your *prayer* request) when you pray, or is there doubt in your heart when you are praying?

2. Do you give God his respect when you pray to Him or do you just rush in with your request or petitions expecting an immediate answer?

3. Are you able to consistently pray day in and day out without fail?

4. Can you live in the expectation and act like you already got what you asked God for?

5. Are you willing to devote at least one hour a day to God in *prayer*?

6. Are you willing to commit to praying in the hierarchy format presented in this chapter?

7. Do you pray in and speak in other tongues? If not, are you willing to find someone to endow you with Holy Spirit and assist you in speaking the official language of the kingdom of God? *(See References for further instructions).*

NOTES

SPIRITUAL PRINCIPLE #3
Just Be... A Time of Preparation (There is a reason for everything that happens in your life)

> *It is better to be prepared for an opportunity and not have one,*
> *Than to have an opportunity and not be prepared!*
>
> **Whitney Young**

PREPARATION

BIBLICAL REFERENCE:
To every thing there is a season and a TIME to every purpose under the heaven.

Ecclesiastes 3:1KJV

Go to now, ye that say, To day or to morrow we will go into such a city, and continue there a year, and buy and sell, and get gain: Whereas ye know not what shall be on the morrow. For what is your life? It is even a vapour, that appeareth for a little time, and then vanisheth away. For that ye ought to say, If the Lord will, we shall live, and do this, or that.

James 4:13-15 KJV

I have often wondered (and said), okay God, since this business was your idea (purpose) that you gave to me (vision), then why am I having such a difficult time making it...

▼ *A Reality*...(then once it was a reality)...
▼ *A Success*...(then once it was a success)...
▼ *Prosperous Enterprise*...(this is where preparation begins)

Success occurs when opportunity meets *preparation*. An effective person gets up early in the morning to *prepare* for the day. I know some people who get up as early as 4:00 a.m. to start their day.

To *Prepare* is to *procure; make ready beforehand for some purpose, to use or activity; work out the details of; plan in advance; to put together or compound; put into written form; or to get ready.*

If you are wondering why it is so important to get up early before you begin your work, here is an example of what would consist of an early morning person's routine:

▼ ***Pray*** - As soon as you get up begin your day communicating with God to set the right course of your day.

▼ ***Exercise*** – Your body needs to be healthy and fit for the long work hours you will endure. I have found that mental labor is more taxing on the body than physical labor. *(See the section on Your Personal Life in Spiritual Principle #6).*

▼ ***Eat*** – Your spiritual and physical body needs food. Your spiritual food is listening to tapes or watching Christian programs of spiritual authorities you can glean from. Your physical food is a wholesome and balanced meal that keeps you alert and active. Breakfast truly is the most important meal of the day.

▼ ***Read*** – It is important to know what is going on in the world around you. Reading the daily newspaper, business and industry magazines, and watching news channel programs provide tremendous information for you and the clients you will serve.

Have you heard of the famous cliché that says, *"The early bird gets the worm"*? This is what that cliché says to me:

Worm = Food = Substance = Wisdom, Insight & Creativity for Increase = Prosperity
Prosperity (Material possessions. The things that you have been praying for)

When your head is clear after your prayer and devotion time, you are free to receive the *wisdom that dwells with prudence and find out the knowledge of witty inventions and creative ideas. For it is God that teaches you how to profit, and leads you in the way that you should go.*
Proverbs 8:21 and Isaiah 48:17 KJV

It was three years after I had my first office building when I read that an overnight success is 15 years in the making! I also learned that the higher a tree grows, the deeper its roots must grow. In order for me to realize (and wait) for the manifestation of the next level of success for my company, there is a process of *preparation* at each new level. It was not until I was finding the scripture reference for *preparation* that I read Ecclesiastes 3:9-14 which revealed verses 10-11 to me in a new light. In order for me to eat, drink, and enjoy (find satisfaction in all my toil), I must go through the travail He has set before me, to *prepare* me for the next level!

What profit hath he that worketh in that wherein he laboureth? I have seen the travail, which God hath given to the sons of men to be exercised in it. He hath made every thing beautiful in his time: also he hath set the world in their heart, so that no man can find out the work that God maketh from the beginning to the end. I know that there is no good in them, but for a man to rejoice, and to do good in his life. And also that every man should eat and drink, and enjoy the good of all his labour, it is the gift of God.

Ecclesiastes 3:9-14 KJV

At the end of a long workday, laborious project, or finally satisfying that unruly customer - Rejoice! You have just received the necessary experience you will need for the next level of your business. It might not make sense as to the reason why you had to endure that awful experience but in the end, that experience works together for your good and the good of your company! It is a gift from God to know that you have successfully overcome your trial. It is a gift of God to receive the necessary labor to make you strong, to pass the test, and to obtain the satisfaction of God's grace. This is enough for me to take myself out for a good meal. Remember to celebrate each goal you accomplish!

Of course when you are starting out with your business idea, or when you are going through rough times, you don't see trials as a gift. You don't see trials as beautiful. You don't see the end from the beginning. This is where you have to trust God when you cannot trace (see) Him. God has appointed every promise in your life to have a due season. At the highest point of your frustration and the temptation to quit is the very point or next step when your due season arrives. The appointed time is the manifestation of the blessing you have been waiting for.

The preparations of the heart in man, and the answers of the tongue, is from the LORD. All the ways of a man are clean in his own eyes, but the LORD weigheth the spirits.

Proverbs 16:1-2 KJV

Mortals make elaborate plans, but God has the last word. Humans are satisfied with whatever looks good; God probes for what is good.

Proverbs 16:1-2 The Message

During this season of *preparation* is the time to learn how to take the frustration out of your life. Now is the time for you to prepare yourself to make these next seven steps towards your due season. Although you may have your purpose, vision, and goals written down all in order, you have to allow God to prune you and shape your business idea in the way that He purposed them to be manifested.

Now is the time to study each word and see how your business idea measures up to the meanings of these words. This is an exercise that can be done on a yearly basis as your company grows. Now is the time for you to ***Just Be...***

BIBLICAL REFERENCE:

There's an opportune time to do things, a right time for everything on the earth.

Ecclesiastes 3:1 The Message

And now I have a word for you who brashly announce, "Today—at the latest, tomorrow—we're off to such and such a city for the year. We're going to start a business and make a lot of money." You don't know the first thing about tomorrow. You're nothing but a wisp of fog, catching a brief bit of sun before disappearing. Instead, make it a habit to say "If the Master wills it and we're still alive, we'll do this or that."

James 4:13-15 The Message

PREPARATION QUESTIONS:

1. Are you willing to set a daily routine to get up early and properly prepare yourself on a daily basis?

2. Are you willing to make the necessary adjustments to what you eat (spiritually and physically), read and do for your body?

3. Are you willing to let God into your business affairs to prune and modify those things that need to be changed?

4. Are you ready and willing to go through the process and be changed?

SPIRITUAL PRINCIPLE #3
Just Be... A Time of Preparation (There is a reason for everything that happens in your life)

> *When you leave your "Comfort Zone", it is not by your choice,*
> *but by the Will of God.*
> *There is a difference between a contribution and a sacrifice.*
> *What we think is a sacrifice, is really a contribution to God.*
>
> *Carla A. Nelson*

COMMITTED

BIBLICAL REFERENCE:
Commit thy works unto the Lord, and thy thoughts shall be established. The Lord hath made all things for himself; yea, even the wicked for the day of evil.
Proverbs 16:3-4 KJV

When you are deciding whether or not to plunge ahead and go forward with your business idea (vision), there are many people, situations, and yes, your own thoughts, that will ask and test you to see just how *committed* you will be to make your vision become a reality. The old saying, *"When the going gets tough, the tough get going"* can also be translated another way by saying, *"You've got to be committed to the cause"*. Starting and maintaining a company on a full time basis will take sacrifice, hard work, long hours, and commitment. You need to ask yourself how bad do you really want to do it and do you have what it takes to see the vision become a reality. The advantage you have as a citizen in the kingdom of God is that you already have all the necessary resources from God (who is your source) required for your success. When you follow God's plan for your business idea and obligate yourself to His righteous commitment, God through Jesus Christ promises to give you what you need to see it to completion. This is the first step in keeping company with God.

Many people say they know it is going to take a lot of hard work and long hours to start and maintain their business idea. Unless that person has run a company or lived with someone who owned their own company, they have no idea just how much commitment is required.

To *Commit* is to *connect; entrust; to put into charge or trust; to cosign or record for preservation. To carry into action deliberately, obligate, or bind. To pledge or assign to some particular course or use, or to reveal the views of a person on the issue.*

As you work on your business idea you will have many obstacles along the way. Being *committed* means you have to find ways to overcome obstacles. You need to see obstacles as an occasion to learn something new or an opportunity for your company to grow up and mature! Again, looking at the life of Joseph, you notice he was *committed* to the vision God gave him and to the people he served regardless of his current situation:

But he refused, and said unto his Master's wife, behold, my master wrotteth not what is with me in the house, and he hath committed all that he hath to my hand. And the keeper of the prison committed to Joseph's hand all the prisoners that were in the prison; and whatever they did there, he was the doer of it.
Genesis 39:8,22 KJV

Joseph was so *committed* to follow God's ways that his master *committed* Joseph to handle to his business affairs. We see the keeper of the prison commit everything to Joseph even though he was a prisoner himself! God's blessings were already on Joseph regardless of his circumstances, even though they could not be seen in the natural. Joseph lived a stress free life even though he was a slave!

In Spiritual Principle #1 on Vision, we stated that a true vision from God is bigger than something you can do on your own. Having a righteous commitment is to obligate yourself to do what God tells you to do in any given situation. It is not an emotional or impulsive commitment for the short term, but more like a process for the long haul.

The *Commitment* process is *the act of committing to a mission, charge or trust; an agreement or pledge to do something in the future; something pledged, or the state of being obligated or emotionally impelled.*

True leaders are people who lead by example. They serve as a visible model of someone who is *committed* to a course of action. They need to be in order to get others to believe in their idea, vision, or strategy. *Committed* Leaders are characterized by:

▼ **The smile on their face and the positive outlook they have whether things are going good or not so good with their plans for the business.**

▼ **The reputation for going the second mile when the first mile almost wore them out! They are not quitters.**

▼ **Their focus to meet the needs of the people they serve. Not only in business but also with their family and in the organizations they belong to.**

▼ **Always going the extra mile. Giving people more than they expect to get.**

▼ **Embracing success as lifestyle. They are intentional in their positive outlook on life and about doing the best, not settling for mediocrity.**

▼ **Knowing that being proactive is better than being reactive. They are initiators, forerunners and doers.**

▼ **Their encouraging words especially to others who are going through something that they have been through. Their words are not just superficial; they have meaning because they have "Been there and done that"!**

Committed people are Holy. They are people of integrity, high moral character with pure motives. They live a lifestyle of faith, even when they are in trouble. They are lead by Holy Spirit to guide and direct their steps on a daily basis. Committed people take dominion over the earth, which includes themselves and their surroundings (environment). In Daniel 7:18 it states...*But the saints of the most High shall take the kingdom, and possess the kingdom for ever, even for ever and ever*, which means citizens of the kingdom of God are to take the kingdom (earth) that God gave us to possess just as Adam possessed the Garden of Eden.

And God said, Let us make man in our image, after our likeness: and let them have dominion over the fish of the sea, and over the fowl of the air, and over the cattle, and over all the earth, and over every creeping thing that creepeth upon the earth.

Genesis 1:26 KJV

And the LORD God took the man, and put him into the garden of Eden to dress it and to keep it.

Genesis 2:15 KJV

God *committed* to you by giving you the purpose and vision for your life before you were born. Your commitment to God is to seek, pursue and implement that vision during your lifetime. You have to *commit* to your vision when no one else believes in you but you! Being *committed* is not a destiny but a journey and surpasses the season of preparation. It is continual throughout the life of your company.

BIBLICAL REFERENCE:
Put God in charge of your work, then what you've planned will take place. God made everything with a place and purpose; even the wicked are included- but for judgment.

Proverbs 16:3-4 The Message

COMMITTED QUESTIONS:

1. Just how bad do you want your business idea to become a successful company?

2. How much of your time, energy, resources and money are you willing to sacrifice?

3. Do others consider you a leader? *If not, how can you expect others to work with you or follow you?*

4. Do others consider you a person who is committed to someone else's idea? *If not, how can you expect others to be committed to your idea?*

5. Are you a person who starts hobbies, sports, or other projects but don't complete them because you lost interest in them? *If so, how can you expect others to finish your projects?*

6. Are you a person who does not complete projects that are not yours, therefore, "you have nothing at stake" if it is not completed? *If so, how can you expect others to complete your projects or commit to your business ideas?*

SPIRITUAL PRINCIPLE #3
Just Be… A Time of Preparation (There is a reason for everything that happens in your life)

The Elements for being Focused are to be
Disciplined in your Lifestyle
Determined in your Thinking and
Directed in your Actions.

Carla A. Nelson

FOCUSED

BIBLICAL REFERENCE:
Keep thy heart with all diligence; for out of it are the issues of life. Put away from thee a froward mouth, and perverse lips put far from thee. Let thine eyes look right on, and let thine eyelids look straight before thee. Ponder the path of thy feet, and let all thy ways be established. Turn not to the right hand nor to the left: remove thy foot from evil.

Proverbs 4:23-27 KJV

God gave me a purpose to do His Will in a certain amount of time - it is called *My Lifetime.* I have seen the vision for my life. I know what my purpose is, professionally and personally. I have separated my goals and objectives into tasks and placed them in a plan of action. I have seen the completion of my project or my purpose in life with everything laid out for me, and it looks great! So why do I get off track as I journey down life's path? Why do I get distracted with things that are not part of the plan? Why is it taking me so long to finish each task? Is it because I am not *focused*? Is it because I am distracted? If so, what is it I must do to get back on track or on the right path? The answers to these questions can be found in a devotional I heard from Elder Brenda J. Haliburton. To remain *focused* you must daily **Praise, Prepare, Plan,** and **Press.**

▼ **Praise** God for who He is and what He does, for He daily loads you with benefits and provisions for your life. *The LORD is my strength and my shield; my heart trusted in him, and I am* *helped: therefore my heart greatly rejoiceth; and with my song will I praise him. Palm 28:7 KJV*

▼ **Prepare** your day to do what is necessary to manage your time wisely. Do not live your life in default. *LORD, thou hast heard the desire of the humble: thou wilt prepare their heart, thou wilt cause thine ear to hear. Psalm 10:17 KJV*

▼ **Plan** the steps (goals) for your company. God cannot help you if you do not have any plans. *The steps of a good man are ordered by the LORD: and he delighteth in his way. Psalm 37:23 KJV*

▼ **Press** on to do whatever it takes to remain; you must hang on in there until the end. There are no rewards for being a quitter. *I press toward the mark for the prize of the high calling of God in Christ Jesus. Philippians 3:14 KJV*

We define *Focus* as *an adjustment so as to form a clear distinct image or vision, the relative clarity of an image, any central point of activity or attraction, or to concentrate.* The word *focus* is not found in the King James Version of the Bible but there are other words used to describe its meaning. The word **Meditate** (to concentrate) is found 14 times. There are times when only concentration will help me *stay* on track and not *stray* off track. The Bible admonishes me to meditate on the word of God, both day and night.

When it comes to completing my tasks, (the ones that are tied into the purpose God gave me), I must meditate on it daily. Meditation allows me to see things clearly and not become distracted. During my quiet time I can *see* what the end of a completed task will look like. This image (part of my vision) is what keeps me *focused.*

This book of the law shall not depart out of thy mouth; but thou shalt meditate therein day and night, that thou mayest observe to do according to all that is written therein: for then thou shalt make thy way prosperous, and then thou shalt have good success.

Joshua 1:8 KJV

But his delight is in the law of the LORD; and in his law doth he meditate day and night. And he shall be like a tree planted by the rivers of water, that bringeth forth his fruit in his season; his leaf also shall not wither; and whatsoever he doeth shall prosper.

Psalm 1:2-3 KJV

The word **Path** is found 23 times in the Bible. To follow the path, God's path, I must be quiet, patient, and centered. This is the best way to hear the voice of the Lord and allow Holy Spirit to guide me throughout the day. The guidance of Holy Spirit is *so* sweet. He literally *makes my day*! The path He leads me on attracts all the necessary provisions I need for my vision. These provisions are used to formulate the images I saw during my time of meditation. It is on the path that the activities of completing my goals and objectives are met.

The path is where I meet people who have the power, ability, and influence to fulfill the vision. It is where synergy takes place and alliances are built. I can remain focused while walking the path because no matter what distractions come my way, I have already seen the end. In my mind's eye, the vision is finished before I get started.

Thou wilt show me the path of life: in thy presence is fullness of joy; at thy right hand there are pleasures for evermore.

Psalms 16:11 KJV

Make me to go in the path of thy commandments; for therein do I delight. NUN. Thy word is a lamp unto my feet, and a light unto my pathway. I have sworn, and I will perform it, that I will keep thy righteous judgments.

Psalm 119:35,105-106 KJV

But the path of the just is as the shining light, that shineth more and more unto the perfect day.

Proverbs 4:18 KJV

The word **Straightway** is found 42 times. This word is used to describe one that is not deterred for ANY reason. Straightway is an immediate call to action or reaction to a situation. This word is often used in describing the actions or reactions of Jesus during his three-year ministry. Jesus was successful because he was focused. I need to be focused in completing my tasks, and I must *finish them on time*! If I am late or I do not finish my goals and objectives, I have sinned in the eyes of God. He only gave me a limited amount of time to fulfill my purpose. I am supposed to die empty. My purpose is for my *lifetime,* not my *life eternal.*

And Jesus, when he was baptized, went up straightway out of the water: and, lo, the heavens were opened unto him, and he saw the Spirit of God descending like a dove, and lighting upon him: And lo a voice from heaven, saying, This is my beloved Son, in whom I am well pleased.
Matthew 3:16 –17 KJV

And he saith unto them, Follow me, and I will make you fishers of men. And they straightway left their nets, and followed him.
Matthew 4:19-20 KJV

Saying unto them, Go into the village over against you, and straightway ye shall find an ass tied, and a colt with her: loose them, and bring them unto me. And if any man say ought unto you, ye shall say, The Lord hath need of them; and straightway he will send them.
Matthew 21:2-3 KJV

Our number one priority in life is to seek the kingdom of God. In other words, find out what your purpose is in life and pursue it. No matter what your past has been, realize with Jesus Christ as your Lord, and Holy Spirit as your guide and comforter, your future can be great! Yes, there will be times when you will be distracted, get off track, and late in completing a task, (I ought to know I got distracted too many times trying to complete this book).

Realize that is the trick of the enemy. It gives him no greater plea-sure than to see God's Will go uncompleted, so don't fall victim to his devices! To remain *focused* is a skill that requires discipline. You must be conscious, alert, and vigilant.

Be sober, be vigilant; because your adversary the devil, as a roaring lion, walketh about, seeking whom he may devour: Whom resist stedfast in the faith, knowing that the same afflictions are accomplished in your brethren that are in the world. But the God of all grace, who hath called us unto his eternal glory by Christ Jesus, after that ye have suffered a while, make you perfect, stablish, strengthen, settle you.

1Peter 5:8-10 KJV

When you find yourself getting off track, distracted, or unable to finish your tasks, take a step back and look at the original vision for your business idea. This will cause you to:

▼ *Make the proper adjustments necessary to get on track with the vision for your business idea.*

▼ *See things clearly again as you did when you first received your vision from God to create a company.*

▼ *Get the proper image back in perspective in your mind of what the end result will look like for your company.*

▼ *Involve yourself in activities pertaining to your purpose and the mission of your company.*

It is important to remember that other people are waiting on you to fulfill your purpose (starting your company) so they can be satisfied. Your products and services are designed to meet the needs of others. You will never accomplish your goals, actualize the vision, and obtain a successful company if you are not *focused*, and you cannot afford that to happen.

BIBLICAL REFERENCE:

Keep vigilant watch over your heart; that's where life starts. Don't talk out of both sides of your mouth; avoid careless banter, white lies, and gossip. Keep your eyes straight ahead; ignore all sideshow distractions. Watch your step, and the road will stretch out smooth before you. Look neither right or left; leave evil in the dust.

Proverbs 4:23-27 The Message

FOCUS QUESTIONS:

1. Are you easily distracted when you have an important assignment to do?

2. Do you allow time to meditate on God's word on a daily basis? *This is different than your prayer time.*

3. Do you allow God to direct your path in your personal life? *If not, how do you expect him to direct your path in your business life?*

4. Are you able to make the necessary adjustments immediately or *turn on a dime* when God tells you to?

5. Are you involved in activities or organizations that pertain to your purpose or because it looks good on your resume?

SPIRITUAL PRINCIPLE #3
Just Be... A Time of Preparation (There is a reason for everything that happens in your life)

All men commend patience,
Although few be willing to practice it

Thomas A. Kemps

PATIENT

BIBLICAL REFERENCE:
Surely oppression maketh a wise man mad; and a gift destroyeth the heart. Better is the end of a thing than the beginning thereof: and the patient in spirit is better than the proud in spirit. Be not hasty in thy spirit to be angry: for anger resteth in the bosom of fools. Say not thou, What is the cause that the former days were better than these? For thou dost not inquire wisely concerning this.

Ecclesiastes 7:7-10 KJV

You cannot lose patience while waiting on the promises of God regarding your business idea. You can no longer go back to the way things used to be once you have made the commitment to pursue your vision. To be *patient* is part of the preparation process. Being inpatient or hasty is doing things in your own strength. Impatience will cause you to jump the gun or get off track by getting in front of God. Missing the mark is the true meaning of sin. Missing the mark is not doing what God told you to do when He told you to do it.

To be *Patient* is to *bear pains or trials calmly without complaint; to Manifest forbearance under provocation or strain. It is not hasty, impetuous, difficulty or adversity but it is steadfast despite opposition. It is one who is able or wills to bear it.* Patience is to *have the capacity or establish a habit of being patient.*

I waited patiently for the LORD; and he inclined unto me, and heard my cry. He brought me up also out of an horrible pit, out of the miry clay, and set my feet upon a rock, and established my goings.

Psalm 40:1-2 KJV

I waited and waited and waited for God. At last he looked; finally he listened. He lifted me out of the ditch, pulled me from deep mud. He stood me up on a solid rock to make sure I wouldn't slip.

Psalm 40:1-2 The Message

In Psalm 40:1-2, The Message Bible replaced word Patience with the word WAIT. In today's society people do not want to wait for anything, we want everything NOW. Some people say we are a microwave society and I tend to agree with them. People consider it a bother to wait in line to be served (as in a bank line or the drive through at a fast food restaurant). Other people hate to be placed on hold when they call for customer service even though the telephone number they called is toll free! Not to mention those of us who buy instant food to cook in our instant microwave ovens, to eat in the car as we wait in traffic on the way to work to a job that we have no patience for, and one that has nothing to do with the purpose God has for our life!

In business, we can't wait until we get that first big contract. We can't wait to get our own office space and hang our shingle outside. We can't wait to see the money start rolling in from all the sales contracts we solidified. We can't wait to be successful in the eyes of others. How many of us realize that this is when the real work begins? This is not the time to celebrate and take a break, this is the time to fulfill your orders, accomplish your task and complete all that you told your clients you were going to do and to do it on time!

Waiting is the time God uses to correct us, mature us, prove us, and to complete us. It can be a great asset if you know how to use the time to your advantage. Here is a good way to learn to **WAIT** and be patient:

<u>W</u>ithstand – To endure successfully to stand your guard or hold your ground. You have to know how to stand and what suit to wear (put on) while you are standing. If you are having a problem standing (or waiting), then you are not properly dressed! Ephesians 6:10-15. *(Discussed in more detail in Spiritual Principle #5).*

<u>A</u>nticipate – Deliverance from a negative situation and not getting ahead of God. This is connected to your Hope and Faith. You eagerly wait for the Lord's help as God waits for your anticipation of His help. Psalm 27:13 –14, 130:5.

<u>I</u>ntercede – You should always pray and not give up. If you are praying, you are not giving up. If you are not praying, you are giving up! Always thank God for the manifested results during your prayer time! Luke 18:1, Galatians 6:9-10, Ephesians 3:13-14. *(See the section on Prayer in Spiritual Principle #2).*

<u>T</u>rust – You must trust God when you can't trace Him. God did not say He would explain everything to you beforehand. There is a time and purpose for everything in your life. Psalms 37:5,7, Ecclesiastes 3:1-11. *(See the section on Trust in Spiritual Principle #3).*

The season of patience is also known as the season of pruning. God put your gift in you before you were born. In order to develop your gift God puts you in places that are best for you to grow and mature in that gift. If you are in need of patience you will find yourself in situations that will *try* your measure of patience. Each time you fail that measure will be repeated. Each time you succeed, you will be put in new situations that require a larger measure of patience. Understand that this is a time of learning for you. Like going to school, you might not have liked going through it, but in the end, you received the desired results (finishing or graduating) and the reward (obtaining knowledge and being able to endure anything the devil throws your way).

My brethren, count it all joy when ye fall into divers temptations; Knowing this, that the trying of your faith worketh patience. But let patience have her perfect work, that ye may be perfect and entire, wanting nothing.
James 1:2-4 KJV

Patience: The ability to stand steadfast. To continue to do what you know to do Even though in the visible (natural) it doesn't appear that anything is working for you.
Dr. Charles Phillips

Regardless of the number of people who laugh at your business idea, the amount of money you don't have, the people who said they would do business with you but changed their mind, the creditors that call you for a payment you can't make, or endless days when the phone does not ring with good news of a business deal, know that God's word is true. He will come through for you in time, every time. When you can't see how, when, or where God will show up to resolve all of your questions, problems and issues, you have to know, trust and believe in God that He will do what He said He would do.

BIBLICAL REFERENCE:
Brutality stupefies even the wise and destroys the strongest heart. Endings are better than beginnings. Sticking to it is better than standing out. Don't be quick to fly off the handle, Anger boomerangs. You can spot a fool by the lumps on his head. Don't always be asking where are the good old days? Wise folks don't ask questions like that.

Ecclesiastes 7:7-10 The Message

PATIENT QUESTIONS:

1. Are you easily angered when things don't go the way you planned them?

2. Do you question God why you have to wait for something you think you need or deserve now?

3. Do you find yourself getting ahead of yourself and missing out on valuable information or opportunities?

4. Do you ask God if He left you because you are going through a difficult time and are waiting on Him to deliver you?

5. Do you find yourself going through the same negative situations that cause you to lose your patience wondering how did you end up in the same scenario again?

SPIRITUAL PRINCIPLE #3
Just Be… A Time of Preparation (There is a reason for everything that happens in your life)

> *To go to a place of failure and trying it again.*
> *To remain unchanged or fixed on a specified character, condition, or position*
> *To exist past an expected or normal period of time.*
> *To be insistent in the repetition or pressing of an utterance*
> *(as a question or an opinion)*
> *Are the qualities of a Persistent person.*
>
> **Dr. Myles Munroe**

PERSISTENT

BIBLICAL REFERENCE:
And he spake a parable unto them to this end, that men ought always to pray, and not to faint; Saying, There was in a city a judge, which feared not God, neither regarded man: And there was a widow in that city; and she came unto him, saying, Avenge me of mine adversary. And he would not for a while: but afterward he said within himself, Though I fear not God, nor regard man; Yet because this widow troubleth me, I will avenge her, lest by her continual coming she weary me. And the Lord said, Hear what the unjust judge saith. And shall not God avenge his own elect, which cry day and night unto him, though he bear long with them? I tell you that he will avenge them speedily. Nevertheless when the Son of man cometh, shall he find faith on the earth?
Luke 18:1-8 KJV

You have to be a *persistent* person to be in business for yourself. There will be times when you must become your own advocator, motivator, cheerleader, and defender. Remember you are the new kid on the block, so your competitors are going to see what you and your business product or service is made of. You will have to prove yourself every day and fight for your business against those who would want to destroy your idea (including the devil). You will never stop fighting for the survival of your company in the spiritual or natural realm. You will never outgrow the fighting process; you will just learn how to fight better. *(We will discuss fighting for your business in the Appearance Matters section in Spiritual Principle #5).*

To be *Persistent* is to *continue to exist in spite of interference or treatment; exist longer than usual time or continuously as retained beyond the usual period, or to continue without change in a function or structure.* You must stand for what you believe in when others doubt you. To be bold, daring and courageous are characteristics of a *persistent* person. You will have to have a fire inside of you that carries you through persecution and ridicule. You might hear statements like the following:

'Girl! Why do you want to go do something foolish as going into business for yourself? You know that idea of yours will never work. What you need to do is get yourself a better job because no woman will ever succeed doing that'!

'Man, what's wrong with you? Don't you know you have a family to support and bills to pay? How do you expect to take care of them and spend money on trying to get this business off the ground'?

Don't feel bad feel great because you are in good company. The following people in the Bible had to endure persecution and ridicule for their belief in God or what He told them He would do for them. Realize that they praised God throughout the process:

▼ *Jacob's Blessing From God* – Genesis Chapters 28 – 30. *Persistent* to work 14 years for Rachel whom he loved, to become his wife. He honored, praised and worshipped God to the end and he received a vision (business idea) from God that made him rich at the expense of his adversary.

▼ *The Three Hebrew Boys* – Daniel Chapter 3. *Persistent* to stand for the living God and not bow down to the idol of King Nebuchadnezzar. (In our day this would mean to bow down to the world's system).

▼ *Daniel & the Lion's Den* – *Daniel Chapter 6. Persistent* in continuing his daily prayer and devotion to God regardless of the decree the presidents and princes convinced King Darius to sign that would land him in the Lion's den to die.

▼ *Nehemiah* – Chapter 4: Sanballat and Tobiah. *Persistent* to build the wall of Jerusalem regardless of naysayers. For there is always someone who will nag you enough to quit what God told you to finish.

▼ *Paul* – The Book of Acts. *Persistent* to preach the Gospel of Jesus Christ regardless of how many times he was beaten, imprisoned and threatened with death. He finished is purpose in life!

Do you have the tenacity to constantly talk to people who don't want to listen to your great idea or sell to those who don't want to buy your product? How many "NO's" are you willing to endure before you receive a "YES"? Good sales people will tell you that it is just a matter of time, usually the next sales call or visit before someone will say yes to what they are selling. *Persistent* people do not blame others for their faults, mistakes or errors. They do not look at failure and quit, they learn from their mistakes or shortcomings, make the necessary adjustments, press on and keep going.

Persistent people control their environment. They are not concerned about how they look while getting what belongs to them. They insist on having what they are going after and will irritate the opposition until they get what they want or until the opposition leaves. In other words, they will stand up against opposition until they wear it out!

When times get tough for them and it looks like they are about to fall 1000 feet, Persistent people tie a knot at the end of their rope and hang on until their change comes. *Persistent* people make other people who are against them so tired of resisting them they either become their friends, allies, or at least give them the respect they deserve.

Persistent people are not quitters the only way they give up is after they are finished! Some people may say you are nagging, demanding, stubborn or dogged. Don't let it bother you. You are determined (which is another word for purpose) about getting what you deserve; what is rightfully yours. Think of the Bulldog. The nose of a bulldog is bent backwards so he can breathe while he bites and bears down on his victim. He does not let go until his victim gives up, leaves or dies. So remember the next time when it gets rough pursuing your business idea, or accomplishing one of your goals, be like the Bulldog…Bite, Breathe, and Bear down!!!

BIBLICAL REFERENCE:

Jesus told them (the disciples) a story showing that it was necessary for them to pray consistently and never quit. He said, "There was once a judge in some city who never gave God a thought and cared nothing for people. A widow in that city kept after him: 'My rights are being violated. Protect me!' He never gave her the time of day. But after this went on and on he said to himself, "I care nothing what God thinks, even less what people think. But because this widow won't quit badgering me, I'd better do something and see that she gets justice-otherwise I'm going to end up beaten black and blue by her pounding.'" Then the Master said, "Do you hear what that judge, corrupt as he is, is saying? So what makes you think God won't step in and work justice for his chosen people, who continue to cry out for help? Won't he stick up for them? I assure you, he will. He will not drag his feet. But how much of that kind of persistent faith will the Son of Man find on the earth when he returns?

Luke 18:1-8 The Message

PERSISTENT QUESTIONS:
1. Do you give up when things become too difficult, especially when it hurts (emotionally, physically and financially)?

2. How long are you willing to work for the love of your business and to become rich?

3. Are you willing to go through the fire (trials, errors, seasons of no income, loss of clients & customers) for what you believe in, even if it looks like the death of your business?

4. Have you counted the costs of what it will take to constantly pursue your business regardless of those who would try to plot against you, kill your reputation and/or your business?

5. Jesus is the author and finisher of our faith. Can you finish what he authored for your life?

SPIRITUAL PRINCIPLE #3
Just Be… A Time of Preparation (There is a reason for everything that happens in your life)

Needs create Purpose which demands Responsibility
The more Responsible you are
The more your Purpose is fulfilled within you.
Elder Leonard Corbin

RESPONSIBLE
*Since the word Responsible or Responsibility is not used in the Bible, the closest word we can use is the word **Account or Accountability**.*

BIBLICAL REFERENCE:
By him therefore let us offer the sacrifice of praise to God continually, that is, the fruit of our lips giving thanks to his name. But to do good and to communicate forget not: for with such sacrifices God is well pleased. Obey them that have the rule over you, and submit yourselves: for they watch for your souls, as they that must give account, that they may do it with joy, and not with grief: for that is unprofitable for you.

Hebrews 13:15 –17 KJV

If you are not able to submit to your current boss or authority figure what makes you think others will want to submit or subject themselves to you when you start your business? In the many jobs I have had, I noted all the things I did not like, such as the way I was treated because of my age, color of my skin, grade of my hair, or the type of clothes I wore. I made mental notes of the unfair policies and procedures some of my employers implemented or how I was talked to when given instructions or corrections regarding my work. I did not like being talked down to so I said I would not do that to my staff.

While you are working for someone else, take note of how you treat your supervisors and authority figures. Do you talk behind their back? Do you discuss issues with them in an adult manner or complain like a child? Do you holler back at your superiors or *buck up* to them when they correct you, or give them the respect they deserve because of the position they hold? (If for no other reason, they do have the power to fire you)!

To be *Responsible* is to be *liable to be called on to answer or to give an account as your primary cause, motive, or agent. To be liable for a legal review or in case with fault or penalties. One who is able to answer for one's conduct or obligations, or one who is reliable or trustworthy. One who is able to choose for oneself between right and wrong. A Burden.*

To be in business for yourself you must be a self-starter. You cannot wait on your boss to tell you what to do because YOU are the boss! God will not even tell you what to do until you start moving! You can no longer wait for your tasks and assignments to be given to you as a handout. You must knock, seek and find out what you need to do in order to have a successful company. It is through the knocking, seeking and finding that you obtain answers to your questions and solutions to your problems.

The word *responsible* is not found in the bible, so we will look at the word **accountable**. It is during your time of adversity, the real you will always show up. When your feet are put to the fire is when others get to see who you really are! You are accountable for all of your actions. The flesh reacts to those things that are uncomfortable. If your spirit man is strong, your flesh will obey the spirit when adversity comes. God does not condone procrastination and is not interested in your excuses, only your results. The reason why you might not have received the manifestation of your blessing is because you are slow to complete the last thing God told you to do! At all times and in all places you must be accountable for your actions or you will face the consequences for the lack thereof. Where there is lack in your life, you are probably slacking in doing what you know you need to do!

And he (Jesus) said also unto his disciples, There was a certain rich man, which had a steward; and the same was accused unto him that he had wasted his goods. And he called him, and said unto him, How is it that I hear this of thee? give an account of thy stewardship; for thou mayest be no longer steward. Then

106

the steward said within himself, What shall I do? for my lord taketh away from me the stewardship: I cannot dig; to beg I am ashamed. I am resolved what to do, that, when I am put out of the stewardship, they may receive me into their houses. And the lord commended the unjust steward, because he had done wisely: for the children of this world are in their generation wiser than the children of light. And I say unto you, Make to yourselves friends of the mammon of unrighteousness; that, when ye fail, they may receive you into everlasting habitations. He that is faithful in that which is least is faithful also in much: and he that is unjust in the least is unjust also in much. If therefore ye have not been faithful in the unrighteous mammon, who will commit to your trust the true riches? And if ye have not been faithful in that which is another man's, who shall give you that which is your own? No servant can serve two masters: for either he will hate the one, and love the other; or else he will hold to the one, and despise the other. Ye cannot serve God and mammon.

Luke 16:1-4,8-13 KJV

Jesus said to his disciples, "There was once a rich man who had a manager. He got reports that the manager has been taking advantage of his position by running up huge personal expenses. So he called him in and said, "What's this I hear about you? You're fired. And I want a complete audit of your books.' "The manager said to himself, 'What am I going to do? I've lost my job as a manager. I'm not strong enough for a laboring job, and I'm too proud to beg...Ah, I've got a plan. Here's what I'll do." Now here's a surprise: The master praised the crooked manager! And why? Because he knew how to look after himself. Streetwise people are smarter in this regard than law-abiding citizens. They are on constant alert, looking for angles, surviving by their wits. I want you to be in the same way – but for what is right. – using every adversity to stimulate you to creative survival, to concentrate your attention on the bare essentials, so you'll live, really live, and not complacently just get by on good behavior." "If you're not honest in small things, you'll not be honest in big things; If you're a crook in small things, you'll be a crook in big things. If you're not honest in small jobs, who will put you in charge of the store? No worker can serve two bosses: He'll either hate the first and love the second or adore the first and despise the second. You can't serve both God and the Bank."

Luke 16:1-4, 8-13 The Message

Another area of being accountable is when it comes to borrowing or taking office supplies for your personal use. If you don't have a clue how much office supplies costs, wait until you run your own office and have to replenish them. You will begin to feel like Mr. Scrooge – counting every pen, pencil and pad, and looking to see who has what in their desk drawer. It might seem funny but office supplies costs and it won't be a laughing matter when you run low of supplies, toner for the copier or printer, copy paper, or office snacks, (because you are running low on funds) and your staff is looking at you wondering why you have not restocked the supply cabinet!

The phrase *Time is Money* is a true statement in the world of business. When you take things that belong to your employer, return to your desk late from your break, or arrive late and leave early, you cost the company money. When your productivity is low, you upset your co-workers for not pulling your weight and most importantly, you are not a good representative of a kingdom citizen. Time is a resource that too many people abuse. It is the one resource in life you cannot get any more of. Money can buy almost anything but time. Once time is gone, it is called the past and you cannot get it back!

As a citizen of the kingdom of God your lifestyle and character should be beyond reproach. If you set good work standard for yourself as an employee, you will set good working standard for your own company. A responsible person is dependable, productive and disciplined. They have integrity. People of integrity are protected by God, get promoted, obtain favor from God and man, and live a peaceful life. People of integrity are free from drama and free from stress. People of integrity also don't have to worry about being put out on the street! Even when evil comes upon them, God will always provide them a way of escape.

Stewards are required to give an account of their work. As the owner of your business you must give an account not only to God but also to the Internal Revenue Service, State Licensing Board, your employees, your customers, and the business community! I attended a business seminar in February 1996. A young man said his reason for wanting to start his own business was to be his own boss. I told him as a business owner or entrepreneur you are never your own boss. When you are the owner of your company, your clients and customers becomes your boss. They tell you what they want, when they want it and how they want it. The only difference is that you get to keep the fruits of your labor (the profit)!

In life you are responsible for the choices you make. So it is in business or having your own company. You are responsible for the choices you make. You are accountable for the decision made by those who work for or with you. As a kingdom citizen you have the advantage with Jesus as your senior partner, Holy Spirit as your guide, and God to keep company with!

BIBLICAL REFERENCE:

Make sure you don't take things for granted and go slack in working for the common good; share what you have with others. God takes particular pleasure in acts of worship – a different kind of sacrifice – that take place in the kitchen and workplace and on the streets. Be responsive to your pastoral leaders. Listen to their counsel. They are alert to the condition of your lives and work under the strict supervision of God. Contribute to the joy of their leadership, not its drudgery. Why would you want to make things harder for them?

Hebrews 13:15-17 The Message

RESPONSIBILITY (ACCOUNTABLE) QUESTIONS:

1. Do you have what it takes to finish your tasks, assignments or client orders effectively and efficiently regardless of what others say about you or tell you what you can't do?

2. Did you search for the necessary materials to complete your task? Are you responsible and on time in completing your assignment or do you give excuses for not having the necessary resources to do the job well?

3. When faced with a challenge or crisis on the job, did you blow up and scream "why does this always happen at the last minute?" or did you pull away to pray and ask God how to handle the situation before responding or taking any action?

4. Are you a person of integrity or do you take office pens, paper clips, note pads, and/or any other office supply (big or small) home thinking it won't be missed or makes large quantities of copies on copier machine?

SPIRITUAL PRINCIPLE #3
Just Be… A Time of Preparation (There is a reason for everything that happens in your life)

Silence is the calm, quiet and tranquil presence of God.
It is in this presence that we find everything we need to both
Be still and to resist anything that would come against us.
Elder Brenda J. Haliburton

SILENT

BIBLICAL REFERENCE:
Unto thee will I cry, O Lord my rock; be not silent to me: lest, If thou be silent to me, I become like them that go down into the pit. Hear the voice of my supplications, when I lift up my hands towards thy holy oracle.
Psalm 28:1-2 KJV

The toughest seasons in life are when you feel that you need to hear from God the most, yet you cannot understand why He won't talk to you. I have come to learn over the years of working for others and being a business owner that during the difficult or tough times is when God is speaking the loudest to me. The reason why I did not hear Him came from not wanting to hear what He was saying, or I could not comprehend what He was saying. This occurred because God was trying to teach me something or move me in a new direction and I did not yet understand.

Silent times from God used to be my season of crying, begging and pleading with God to hurry up and get me out of the negative thing I was going through. Now *silent* times from God is a season where I know He wants me to draw closer to Him so He can show me what new thing He has for me or wants me to do.

To be *Silent* is to *subside, let go, lay, or make no utterance. It is one who is indisposed to speak, not loquacious, or one in prayer. It is free from sound or noise, it performs without utterance; not widely or generally known or appreciated; it lacks spoken dialogue. Silent is also called mute, speechless, still, unspoken, or unpronounced.*

Who will rise up for me against the evildoers? or who will stand up for me against the workers of iniquity? Unless the LORD had been my help, my soul had almost dwelt in silence. When I said, My foot slippeth; thy mercy, O LORD, held me up.

Psalm 94:16-18 KJV

Who stood up for me against the wicked? Who took my side against evil workers? If God hadn't been there for me, I never would have made it. The minute I said "I'm slipping, I'm falling," your love, God took hold and held me fast. When I was upset and beside myself, you calmed me down and cheered me up.

Psalm 94:16-18 The Message

Distractions, distractions, distractions. Distractions are a true enemy to silence. You cannot be productive when you are distracted. When you are busy doing whatever it is you do during the day your brain is bombarded with outside information – most of it noise (sounds & words that have no meaning, senseless shouting, or undesirable sounds you do not listen to but you still hear it). How do you expect God to speak to you with all that pollution going into your ears? I realize there are times when some of my best ideas come to me when I am *silent*.

Many people say they hear God's voice while they are in the shower. It is unfortunate that this is the best time God can get your full attention! As citizens of the kingdom of God we are taught to begin your day with prayer and meditation. This time of devotion is not just to thank God for another day and to make your daily confessions, it is also a time when you hear from God, His what, when, why and how He wants you to conduct your day. Being *silent* is difficult for many people. You don't want to hear what is going on in your head, but to hear from God, you have to push past your own internal noise. Find a place to get quiet and wait to listen for the still small voice that speaks so loud and clear to your spirit. If you don't take time out to get *silent* to hear from God, it won't be long before your plans begin to fray, which will lead to frustration.

Stay Calm - the human mind is not creative when it is hot.
Calmness ushers in creativity.

Carla A. Nelson

The pressures of life, work or family will have you going in multiple directions and can cause you to become frustrated or hot. The mind has to be in a state of readiness to solve problems, lead or delegate others, or implement the daily plans for your company. The business day is a time of action. The time of silence is when you allow yourself to be creative. Successful business people, leaders and ministers carve out time to be alone and create an atmosphere of peace and quiet so that their minds can be free to create, plan, or just plain ole' rest!

One of my mentors used to tell me that entrepreneurs must take a minimum of four vacations a year. It is to be at least a four-day three night get-a-way to a place that has no phone or television in the room. You are prohibited from taking your business paraphernalia with you (the cell phone, pager, radio, alarm clock, or laptop computer). You can write your creative ideas and *stuff* down on a piece of paper or napkin (like when you first got started with this idea). Most of all, do not give the address and phone number to others for them to call you! The reason for this is that entrepreneurs do not work 9-5 with weekends off and get two weeks vacation. You have to plan and build in your own rest periods throughout the year. I know some entrepreneurs who have not taken a vacation or mini get-a-way in 10 years!

You may have to force yourself to relax. Your company will be there with all its pressures, deadlines and challenges just waiting for you when you return. Make this silent time become your time, you and God's time to reflect, commune and have fun. Yes—FUN! You will find God to be really humorous! Make it a time of creativity. The body needs "shut down time" in order to rejuvenate itself throughout the year. As entrepreneurs it is important to get what I call *silent rest*. The kind of rest that allows your brain to not think about anything in particular and your body to do absolutely NOTHING!

If you are not able to take a mini get-a-way vacation, indulge yourself in a nice long hot bath complete with bubbles to soothe your body, and candles in the bathroom (no lights please) with soft music to soothe your mind. This is a relaxing treat for men as well as women. They need it more so than women because they are always in a state of readiness, which makes it difficult for them to relinquish control (even of themselves)!

> *Silence is true wisdom's best reply*
> *Euripides Fragments*

'*Silence is Golden*' our mothers and grandmothers used to say. It is not in the Bible but you would think it was the way they rattled it off to us when we (as children) were making too much noise. Silence is golden because Gold is a precious and somewhat rare mineral that we consider extremely valuable. Silence is something we do not make time to get enough of, therefore it is considered valuable. Anyone who has had to write a paper for school, a proposal for work or your business, or a book (like me) understands the necessity for quiet time – silence; free of distractions, senseless shouting, or words or sounds with no meaning. As you embark on making preparations for your company, schedule in some time of silence to hear from God for yourself.

> *There is an eloquent silence:*
> *It serves sometimes to approve, sometimes to condemn;*
> *There is a mocking silence;*
> *There is a respectful silence.*
> *Francios De La Rochefoucould*

BIBLICAL REFERENCE:
Don't turn a deaf ear when I call you, God. If all I get from you is deafening silence, I'd be better off in the Black Hole. I'm letting you know what I need, calling out for help and lifting my arms toward your inner sanctum.
Psalm 28:1-2 The Message

SILENT QUESTIONS:
1. Are you able to hear from God when times are most difficult?

2. Do you look at your times of silence as a curse or a blessing? How do you spend your times of silence?

3. The answers to questions that trouble me usually come to me in the shower as with most people. When do the answers to your questions come to you?

4. Are you able to take a mini vacation without the business paraphernalia? If not, try it, you might like it!

5. Are you able to carve out times of silence during your current work schedule?

SPIRITUAL PRINCIPLE #3
Just Be... A Time of Preparation (There is a reason for everything that happens in your life)

When you learn to Trust God, you allow yourself to become like Clay so that the Potter (God) can mold you into a beautiful vessel!
Carla A. Nelson

TRUSTING

BIBLICAL REFERENCE:
Blessed is the man that trusteth in the Lord, and whose hope the Lord is. For he shall be as a tree planted by the waters, and that spreadeth out her roots by the river, and shall not see when heat cometh, but her leaf shall be green; and shall not be careful in the year of drought, neither shall cease from yielding.
Jeremiah 17:7-8 KJV

Trust is the main ingredient for the success of any relationship. Your actions and interactions with other people demonstrate *trust*. Your actions and interactions with God demonstrate your *trust* in Him.

Trust exists when you make yourself vulnerable to another whose subsequent behavior you cannot control. To depend on someone to do something for you is a matter of *trust*. When you are willing to consider alternative viewpoints and utilize other people's expertise and abilities to succeed as a group or a team, you exhibit *trust*. As you start and grow your business, you will need to exhibit that same level of trust in God. Trusting God is the reciprocal of being trustworthy. You need to establish *trust* with God first, then He will be able to *trust* you.

To *Trust* is to *be confident; be faithful; believe in; depend upon; rely on the truthfulness or accuracy of something. It is more than true; the assured reliance on the character, ability, strength, or truth of someone or something. One in which confidence is placed.*

Trust in the LORD with all thine heart; and lean not unto thine own under-standing. In all thy ways acknowledge him, and he shall direct thy paths.
Proverbs 3:5-6 KJV

Trust God from the bottom of your heart; don't try to figure out everything on your own. Listen for God's voice in everything you do, everywhere you go; he's the one who will keep you on track.
Proverbs 3:5-6 The Message

Before you decide to *trust* someone else with the vision for your business idea you need to *trust* God and His word. You may not understand everything all at once, including the reason why He gave you the vision. To walk, live and act on what God's word says is to rely on God and hear what He has to say, which can only be done through fellowship with Him. When you learn to do this, it makes the task of building your company and getting others to follow your leadership easy. When you *trust* God you are totally relying on Him and not your limited knowledge and understanding to lead you on the path of success.

Building *trust* with others is always needed when leaders are accomplishing extraordinary things. The foundation of a trusting relationship is to believe that the other person has integrity. Honoring your commitments and keeping your promise demonstrates *trust*. Taking a measure of risk in relating to others and feeling that you will not be injured (emotionally or physically) in the process is what moves others to *trust* you at a new level. *Trust* in a relationship generally develops gradually over time through a course of personal interactions.

To deepen your relationship with God requires taking the initiative in trusting Him despite the uncertainty of the progression of your business idea. If you do not *trust* God in the little things your relationship with Him will remain stalled at a low level of caution and suspicion. You will need to learn how to *trust* God when you cannot trace Him or His ways!

You must learn to *trust* God's direction in leading you on the journey in building your company. *Trust* is not based on feelings, emotions or how things look in the natural. Like God, *trust* is a time-tested attribute. It is built up based on the experiences you go through in life. You will learn to follow God's directions, regardless of the way you feel or how He directs you, you do not direct Him. You may not even like some of the paths He takes you down but realize it is necessary to get to your expected end, which is a successful company.

You must be receptive to new ideas, changes in your goals and objectives, and the suggestions from God. He will lead you in the way you should go only if you *trust* Him. He will not force Himself on you. The path that you take may not be easy but you will be able to handle it because God knows you. He knows that you can endure the tests and trials along the path that are necessary to build you up and mature you. It is part of the process to get you to that expected end – to give you the desire of your heart – the successful company to answer the questions and meet the needs of man in the earth.

May I laugh and not cry
May I leap and not limp
May I sing and not sigh
May I not ask the reason why.
Always remembering to trust in You no matter how I may feel.
I should know you are my true father who loves, protects and heals.
Carla A. Nelson

BIBLICAL REFERENCE:

But blessed is the man who trusts me, God, the woman who sticks with God. They're like trees replanted in Eden, putting down roots near the rivers. Never a worry through the hottest of summers, never dropping a leaf, Serene and calm through droughts, bearing fresh fruit every season.
Jeremiah 14:8 The Message

TRUST QUESTIONS:

1. Do other people consider you a trustworthy person?

2. Are you able to totally trust, rely, and depend upon God for everything (resource) in your life right now?

3. If you are willing to consider the viewpoint of other people, are you willing to consider the viewpoint of God?

4. If you expect to trust other people to assist you with your business idea, can God trust you with all the plans He has for you?

5. Can you trust God even if you cannot trace Him or understand His ways?

The Will Of God

The Will of God will never take you, Where the grace of God cannot keep you, Where the arms of God cannot support you, Where the riches of God cannot supply your needs, Where the power of God cannot endow you.

The Will of God will never take you,

Where the Spirit of God cannot work through you, Where the wisdom of God cannot teach you, Where the army of God cannot protect you, Where the hands of God cannot mold you.

The Will of God will never take you, Where the love of God cannot enfold you, Where the mercies of God cannot sustain you, Where the peace of God cannot calm your fears, Where the authority of God cannot overrule for you.

The Will of God will never take you,

Where the comfort of God cannot dry your tears, Where the Word of God cannot feed you, Where the miracles of God cannot be done for you, Where the omnipresence of God cannot find you.

"Everything happens for a purpose. We must not see the wisdom of it all now but trust and believe in the Lord that everything is for the best."

Unknown Author via E-mail

NOTES

SPIRITUAL PRINCIPLE #4
YOU ARE THE BUSINESS (At the end of the day, all you have is your Reputation)

> *God speaks to your potential*
> *Never to your present situation of who you are!*
> **Dr. Charles Phillips**

YOU ARE THE BUSINESS

BIBLICAL REFERENCE:
Seeth thou a man diligent in his business? He shall stand before kings, he shall not stand before mean men.

> *Proverbs 22:29 KJV*

Throughout this book you may have noticed how I refer to your vision as your *business idea*, and refer to the growth and development of that business idea as your *company*. Many of us will use the words business and company interchangeably but they do have different meanings.

To do business is to perform a purposeful activity with a specific function or role. To do business is to have tasks, objectives, and a mission for the business. To do business is to engage in a commercial activity as a means of livelihood, such as a product or service. To do business is to engage in a commerce, trade, or traffic. The word Business is a word of action requiring time, effort, and something that avoids distraction in order to produce at its maximum effort. YOU *Do Business*!

To have a company is to establish a chartered organization that provides a commercial or industrial enterprise. To have a company is to create a separate entity comprised of associates, companions, or members. To have a company is to engage in business transactions that include commerce, trade, or traffic. The word Company is a word that manages business, requiring rules and regulations to operate properly, and to provide a product or service of the highest quality to its customer. YOU *Have a Company* that does business!

Another way of putting it is, as a kingdom citizen you receive a mandate from God to have dominion over the earth by managing a commercial enterprise that engages in specific purposeful activities that accomplishes its goals and objectives while fulfilling its mission with the resources given by the creator and guided by biblical principles from the word of God to properly operate in the earth to provide a product or service of the highest quality thereby glorifying God and edifying man.

As you do business, whether for your company or someone else's, here are points to remember while conducting your daily transactions:

▼ *Your business will continue to go where invited, and remain where appreciated.*

▼ *Your reputation will continue to be made by many acts, and be lost by one.*

▼ *People will go right on preferring to do business with their friends; make some.*

▼ *Go-givers will become the best of go-getters; learn to do both.*

▼ *The "extra mile" will have no traffic jams; take the road less traveled.*

▼ *Your performance will continue to out sell your promises, under promise and over deliver.*

▼ *Your enthusiasm should be as contagious as ever; it is one habit worth giving to someone else.*

▼ *Your know-how will always surpass their question; obtain knowledge and be ready.*

▼ *Trust, not tricks, will keep your customers loyal; it is easier to keep a customer than to obtain a new one.*

▼ *Quality will quickly be prized as a precious possession; people will gladly pay for it!*

Evaluate your life and consider whether you are living with humility and gratitude,
And honoring the Lord with your attitude and behavior.
Shelly Gross-Wade

Listed below are business anecdotes you can formulate as good business habits as you conduct the business affairs for your company.

BUSINESS ANECDOTES

1. *When you take clients out to dinner, make sure they eat your best fruits.*

   When you purchase fruit, it is suggested, depending upon the fruit, that you should squeeze it, pluck it, hold it, smell it, and if they come in a bunch, taste it to see if it is ripe and fresh. Your customers want to buy the best of anything, so when you are presenting your products and services to them or explaining why they should buy from you, show them just how good your fruit is. Always look and act your best when presenting your idea, product or service to a potential buyer. They are not only buying what you are selling they are buying the person selling it. By nature people are attracted to what they see first. Sight is the strongest of the five senses of the human body. The eyes are the gates to the heart, soul, and mind! Look your best, act your best and be your best all the time.

   One way you do this is by giving them *quality customer service*! Many buyers or purchasing agents will tell you they chose their vendors based on customer service first (relationship) and price second!

But the fruit of the Spirit is love, joy, peace, longsuffering, gentleness, good-ness, faith, meekness, temperance: against such there is no law.

Galatians 5:22-23KJV

But the wisdom that is from above is first pure, then peaceable, gentle, and easy to be entreated, full of mercy and good fruits, without partiality, and without hypocrisy. And the fruit of righteousness is sown in peace of them that make peace.

James 3:17-18KJV

2. *In order to receive, you must first give; even the heathens give good tips. (The Sow and Reap concept)*

So often you will find yourself wanting to be in a position of receiving something from someone. How often do you find yourself wanting to be in a position of giving something to someone? I have observed business people give large tips to waiters and waitresses that provide them with good service. Most of these people are not kingdom citizens but they utilize the kingdom principle of sow and reap on a daily basis. That is why they stay prosperous!

The sow and reap concept also works very well in the business community. Companies give money to non-profit organizations not just so they can use it as tax write off, but because they understand what it means to be a good corporate citizen. Companies want to be recognized by the residents and business community of their town for the good works they do. Their reward comes from the people in that community buying merchandise from their stores and from other businesses want-ing to do business with them.

Everybody wants to do business with a successful and reputable company, so why not your company? Sowing, planting seed, investing, whatever you want to call it, all adds up to the more you sow, the more you grow, the larger the harvest, which results in more revenues and a prosperous company!

In the mean while his disciples prayed him, saying, Master, eat. But he said unto them, I have meat to eat that ye know not of. Therefore said the disciples one to another, Hath any man brought him ought to eat? Jesus saith unto them, My meat is to do the will of him that sent me, and to finish his work. Say not ye, There are yet four months, and then cometh harvest? behold, I say unto you, Lift up your eyes, and look on the fields; for they are white already to harvest. And he that reapeth receiveth wages, and gathereth fruit unto life eternal: that both he that soweth and he that reapeth may rejoice together. And herein is that saying true, One soweth, and another reapeth. I sent you to reap that whereon ye bestowed no labour: other men laboured, and ye are entered into their labours.

John 4:31-38KJV

3. When conducting meetings, start on time; when arriving for your appointments, get there ten minutes early.

When you are in charge of a meeting do not punish those who came on time to wait for those who come late. It sends a signal to the on-time people that they are not important, just as it sends a signal to those who are late that it does not matter if they are late. It also gives the late person the assumption of *'now that they have arrived, the meeting may begin'!* Your integrity and reputation is also built on how you conduct your meetings. I know of some business people who will start the meeting if no one is in the room.

When you set an appointment to meet someone at their office, it is your responsibility to get there at least ten minutes early. It is better for you to wait on them than it is for them to wait for you. Being on time tells the person you are serious about meeting with them and that you are a person of integrity. I have often found myself waiting for someone past the appointed time we were supposed to meet. To keep from being frustrated or annoyed, I take a book to read or make notes of something I was thinking about. I have learned to utilize my time wisely – all of it!

Being late tells the person you do not respect or value their time. If for some reason you are delayed (traffic, accident, got lost), give the person a call to inform them of your situation, they will understand. I know of some people who will give you a 10-minute grace period before they leave if you have not arrived for a meeting with them. They are people who value time as a precious resource. You should too!

Then shall the kingdom of heaven be likened unto ten virgins, which took their lamps, and went forth to meet the bridegroom. And five of them were wise, and five were foolish. They that were foolish took their lamps, and took no oil with them: But the wise took oil in their vessels with their lamps. While the bridegroom tarried, they all slumbered and slept. And at midnight there was a cry made, Behold, the bridegroom cometh; go ye out to meet him. Then all those virgins arose, and trimmed their lamps. And the foolish said unto the wise, Give us of your oil; for our lamps are gone out. But the wise answered, saying, Not so; lest there be not enough for us and you: but go ye rather to them that sell, and buy for yourselves. And while they went to buy, the bridegroom came; and they that were ready went in with him to the marriage: and the door was shut. Afterward came also the other virgins, saying, Lord, Lord, open to us. But he answered and said, Verily I say unto you, I know you not. Watch therefore, for ye know neither the day nor the hour wherein the Son of man cometh.
Matthew 25:1-13 KJV

4. *Be specific in explaining the written goal and objectives, tasks, assignments and responsibilities for the company.*

When working with your team on a project it is important to explain what the goals and objectives are of the project. As we stated in Spiritual Principle #1 goals must be clearly written, well defined, tangible and measurable. You should involve your team in the planning process to get their buy-in so when the problems arise they will remain committed to fix the problem and complete the task. While working with your team there will be times when it will take more than one person to solve the problems. Solving problems requires people you can depend on to identify the problem and resolve the issue. Team members will work on a different part of the project, which can cause disagreements. Don't ignore their opposing view, hear them out, and determine the best method to solve the problem. It just might save you time and money in the end. Realize it is okay to agree to disagree as long as the resolution is a positive one.

A clearly written goal that is measurable is one of the most effective ways to foster collaboration among the team because everyone knows what is expected of them. Your team will remain focused on the goal because they are all going in the same direction. Leave room for them to voice their differences of opinions during meetings. Great minds think alike but they don't always think the same thing at the same time. Your team will appreciate your willingness to hear their point of view, respect you and deepen their level of trust in you.

And I said unto the nobles, and to the rulers, and to the rest of the people, The work is great and large, and we are separated upon the wall, one far from another. In what place therefore ye hear the sound of the trumpet, resort ye thither unto us: our God shall fight for us. So we laboured in the work: and half of them held the spears from the rising of the morning till the stars appeared. Likewise at the same time said I unto the people, Let every one with his servant lodge within Jerusalem, that in the night they may be a guard to us, and labour on the day.

Nehemiah 4:19-22 KJV

5. *Always say WE DID IT when the project is a team effort.*
   When planning what you need your team to accomplish, it is essential that you think in terms of *our* goals and objections. Although you are the leader and God gave you the vision, you still need a team to help you accomplish it. No man or woman who is successful got that way only by themselves. They had help and assistance from a group of people who knew how to get the job done. That group of people helped to make the vision of the visionary a reality. Get your team involved in the strategy process by having strategic planning meetings on a regular basis. People will work better for you when they help plan the strategy and when they have the ability to take ownership of a project. You will only be considered a good leader if you have cooperative followers or team players. When your goals are accomplished, everyone gets the credit because *"we did it together"*. If you fall short of your goals you give them encouragement by saying *"we must try to do a better job the next time"*. Therefore, no one takes all the credit and no one receives all the blame.

And a vision appeared to Paul in the night; There stood a man of Macedonia, and prayed him, saying, Come over into Macedonia, and help us. And after he had seen the vision, immediately we endeavoured to go into Macedonia, assuredly gathering that the Lord had called us for to preach the gospel unto them.

Acts 16: 10-11 KJV

But Jesus said unto them, They need not depart; give ye them to eat. And they say unto him, We have here but five loaves, and two fishes. He said, Bring them hither to me. And he commanded the multitude to sit down on the grass, and took the five loaves, and the two fishes, and looking up to heaven, he blessed, and brake, and gave the loaves to his disciples, and the disciples to the multitude. And they did all eat, and were filled: and they took up of the fragments that remained twelve baskets full. And they that had eaten were about five thousand men, beside women and children.

Matthew 14:16-21 KJV

These business anecdotes are a great way to build your reputation among your business colleagues, your team *(see the section on The Red Team in Spiritual Principle #7)*, and the business community at large. They are also good habits to have as you develop and as your company grows. (Discuss in more detail *Your Personal Life in the section on Counting The Cost in Spiritual Principle #6.*)

BIBLICAL REFERENCE:
Observe people who are good at their work – skilled workers are always in demand and admired, they don't take a back seat to anyone.

Proverbs 22:29 The Message

YOU ARE THE BUSINESS QUESTIONS:

1. Do you present your best to others at all times? Do you provide quality customer service at your present job, volunteer organization or ministry group?

2. Do you give good tips when you eat at restaurants, get your hair done, your shoes shined, when the skycap takes your bags at the airport, or when the maid at the hotel cleans your room?

3. Do you have good time management skills? Do you arrive to meetings or appointments on time or are you one who has to make a grand entrance?

4. Are you able to write down your goals and objectives that are clear, well defined and measurable? *If not, re-read Goals in Spiritual Principle #1.*

5. Are you able to tell others "we did it" when working on a team project or do you like to take all the credit only when the project is a success?

SPIRITUAL PRINCIPLE #4
YOU ARE THE BUSINESS (*At the end of the day, all you have is your Reputation*)

*All things and every creation in the earth is God's property.
We should count it a privilege to Possess His things and Manage His creation.*

Carla A. Nelson

THE GOOD STEWARD

BIBLICAL REFERENCE:
And the Lord said, Who then is that faithful and wise steward, whom his lord shall make ruler over his household, to give them their portion of meat in due season? Blessed is that servant, whom his lord when he cometh shall find so doing. Of a truth I say unto you that he will make him ruler over all that he hath.

Luke 12:42-44 KJV

As a citizen of the kingdom of God you are responsible for the gift God has given you in starting your business idea. How you manage that gift is up to you. During the Season of Preparation you learned eight attributes that are essential in starting your business while seeking God for guidance. These attributes are also essential to you, the *good steward* (business owner) as you manage your company and do business with your customers.

A *Good Steward* is faithful to their company to make sure it operates in decency and in order. Accurate financial records are kept on the company. They contribute their time and talent to non-profit organizations, they give financially to their church and community organizations, and they provide sound consultation to other business owners in search of sound advice. *Good Stewards* needs to be:

▼ *Prepared to perform your work in a spirit of excellence*

▼ *Committed to your clients for the work they are paying you to do*

▼ *Focused on your goals to complete them on time with measurable results*

▼ *Patient with yourself, your clients, customers, and the company as plans change*

▼ *Persistent in completing your goals and setting policies and procedures for the company to follow*

▼ *Responsible in keeping your word and getting involved in the business community*

▼ *Silent when listening to God and your customers; their suggestions can be valuable*

▼ *Trusting of others because you cannot become successful all by yourself*

A *good steward* is able to manage their time, money and resources. *Good Stewards* are not wasteful, lazy or abusive with their resources. They value time, both theirs and their customers. They open and close their business on time and return their phone calls within a 48-hour period unless the answering machine indicates otherwise. They can give an account for their actions and expenses, and they can be trusted to get the job done right. *Good Stewards* come highly recommended to others from those they have worked for.

Being a *good steward* is also being responsible for your reputation. Since you are the business, your reputation is built upon the words you speak and the work you do. It is wise to be courteous to everyone. Since you don't know who knows who realize that the person you were mean, nasty or arrogant to could be the one that has a personal relationship with the potential client you want to do business with. When meeting people it is important to keep in mind that they could be the connection to your next referral, reference, client, or contract!

Being a *good steward* also means your word becomes your bond and the quality of your work should be one of excellence. If an error is made, or the customer is not satisfied with their purchase, you are the one who has to make it right. A *good steward* takes responsibility for errors made and does what is necessary to correct it. You don't blame someone else when something goes wrong. People understand that mistakes happen, but how you handle it is what makes the difference. *The buck does stop with you,* since you own the company! Neither God nor your customers will tolerate the blame game or excuses. God does not condone procrastination and is not interested in your excuses He is only interested in your results. The same goes for your customers!

In marketing and sales class we were taught that it is easier and cheaper to keep a customer than it is to get a new customer. If you have good customer service skills and perform quality work, your customers will stay with you and refer you to their friends and business colleagues. When your work and service is of quality, price is not an option. People will pay more for quality and good service. If you are not a *good steward* your customers will notice that you do not value them (and God will too). Eventually the phone will stop ringing, people will stop coming in the door, the money will stop flowing and you will be OUT OF BUSINESS. Make sure you are found by God and your customers to be a *good steward.* One who will not abuse the gift God gave you and will not abuse the customers God sends to you!

BIBLICAL REFERENCE:
The Master said, "Let me ask you; Who is the dependable manager, full of common sense, that the master puts in charge of his staff to feed them well and on time? He is a blessed man if when the master shows up he's doing his job.
Luke 12:42-44 The Message

THE GOOD STEWARD QUESTIONS:

1. Are you a good manager of your time, money, resources, and material possessions?

2. Are you a good steward of the gift God gave you?

3. Are you willing to take responsibility for errors made by others or do what it takes to satisfy your customers? Even if it means giving them their money back?

4. What is your personal reputation like? If you don't know, ask someone that will give you an honest answer.

5. Do you have good customer service skills? Do others consider you to be friendly and helpful?

SPIRITUAL PRINCIPLE #4
YOU ARE THE BUSINESS (At the end of the day, all you have is your Reputation)

Your faith is expressed in Planning
Planning is the evidence of your faith
Planning without works is Failure.

Dr. Charles Phillips

PLANNING

BIBLICAL REFERENCE:
Hear counsel, and receive instruction, that thou mayest be wise in thy latter end. There are many devices in a man's heart; nevertheless the counsel of the LORD, that shall stand.

Proverbs 19:20-21 KJV

"If you fail to plan, then you plan to fail". We have all heard this cliché before but it is so true in the life of starting your company. Proper *planning* pulls the promises of God for your business idea out of the spirit realm (eternity) into the earth realm (time). Plans document your vision and bring manifestation to your purpose.

Plans are *a foundation or a fixed in place. They are a method for achieving an end; procedures; an aim towards a goal; designs; to arrange the parts of; to devise or project the realization or achievement of a program, a method devised for making or doing something or attaining an end.*

Planning documents your vision and set in motion the goals and objectives of your company. Without plans your life has no definition and your company has no goal control. Your plans must be:

▼ *Conceived Thoughts*
▼ *Documented and Written*
▼ *Worked Out and Implemented*

Before you start your company you must count the cost during the *planning* process. First, sit down and decide what you want to do, and then consider what it will take to complete what you want to start. If the idea makes sense, if you provide adequate time to do it, if you have identified the proper resources, and if the cost of operation is reasonable, then you are on your way to successfully implementing the business idea you want to start. This is not to say that you will have everything you need to implement your business idea when you start, you just need to obtain as much knowledge and information as you can about what it is you want to do. It is one thing to forecast enough revenue to afford leasing office space for your company but if you expect to build a skyscraper on an office lease budget, you have not counted your costs correctly!

If you do not have a plan you cannot change a plan. Your plans can and will be changed as your company grows but your purpose for the company will not change. Believe me when I say, there will be times when God will scrap your plans and you will wonder if you are doing the right thing. (This is one of those times when you will need to be silent and listen for God's new direction). Just remember that your plans will change, and change, and change, but you must keep your purpose before you and stay focused on the vision at all times because the purpose and the vision does not change. Proverbs 16:1-9 gives clear instructions on how to develop good plans:

▼ *The plans belong to me, the payment belongs to God.* The preparations of the heart in man, and the answer of the tongue, is from the LORD. Proverbs 16:1

▼ *Check your motives.* All the ways of a man are clean in his own eyes, but the LORD weighs the spirits. Proverbs 16:2

▼ *Commit your plans to God.* Commit thy works unto the Lord, and thy thoughts shall be established. Proverbs 16:3

▼ *God will work everything out for you, even the attacks of the wicked.* The Lord hath made all things for himself: yea, even the wicked for the day of evil. Proverbs 16:4

▼ ***Don't be proud.*** Everyone that is proud in heart is an abomination to the Lord: though hands join in hand, he shall not be unpunished. Proverbs 16:5

▼ ***Keep your life on target; Live right and depart from evil.*** By mercy and truth iniquity is purged, and by the fear of the LORD men depart from evil. Proverbs 16:6

▼ ***God will make your enemies your friends.*** When a man's ways please the Lord, he maketh even his enemies to be at peace with him. Proverbs 16:7

▼ ***Don't do anything unjust.*** Better is a little with righteousness than great revenues without right. Proverbs 16:8

▼ ***If you have no plan, God has nothing to direct.*** A man's heart deviseth his way: but the LORD directeth his steps. Proverbs 16:9

Dr. Myles Munroe

As you journey on the path of implementing your business idea plan to make changes to all that you hold dear, especially material possessions. Expect God to tell you to let go of what is comfortable to you and step out of your comfort zone. It is only at this point that you will be able to work the plan – God's Plan!

The first mention of a plan is found in Genesis 11:6, when the people decided "as one" to build the Tower of Babel. Pharaoh of Egypt also mentions *planning* in preparation for the seven-year famine. In Genesis 41:29 – 34, when Joseph was able to interpret Pharaoh's dream, the people had enough food to last through the famine and Joseph was promoted to oversee the rations of it all. A planner is always promoted because they are self –motivated, prepared, and the quality of their work is one of excellence. The entire chapter of Proverbs 16 is God's Instructions to you personally. It speaks to your preparations (plans) in verse 1, your ways (plans) in verse 7, your directions (plans) in verse 9, and getting wisdom (plans) in verse 16.

When you have good plans you can take advantage of any good opportunity that comes your way. Opportunity is like the wind; it comes at will. It does not knock but it stands silently by and waits to be recognized. You have to be ready for opportunity to come at anytime. Normally it goes unnoticed because initially it looks like an unfair exchange. Most people do not recognize opportunity because in order to take advantage of opportunity, you will first have to give up something. Opportunity may look like you are in a place of loss and no one wants to lose!

If you have properly prepared your plans you are ready for opportunity. When the wind blows in opportunity you will be carried away and soar to higher heights (to the next level) with the vision for your company.

When plans are properly prepared provisions quickly come. Provisions are the information, people and resources you need to be successful and prosperous. **Provision** is broken down in two words:

>   **PRO**   In favor of, forward, in place of substitute for, prior situated in front of
>
> **VISION**   The ability to see the end from the beginning, the ability to perceive, discern, or anticipate, foresight, it is bigger than your life (*that is why you need provisions!*)

The way to succeed in business is to have an uncompromising resolve to follow a well thought out plan. You must exert the maximum effort of placing a demand on your available resources to overcome every obstacle and to operate in excellence in order to obtain the predetermined success for your company in such a manner that it glorifies God.

▼ *The power to define (plan) what you want for your company is the power to determine success.*

▼ *The pursuit of the planning and development stage of your business life should be based from a position of contentment,*

and not competition, in order to live your life to the glory of God.

▼ *The pursuit of your visions, dreams and goals will lead to abundance in your life and the life of your company.*

The Seven Dynamic D's

The vision you have for a company (business idea) came from God, therefore, it is your responsibility to fine-tune it. The **Dream** (vision) you have for your business idea will become a true **Desire** when you **Document** the idea on paper. You should be able to **Describe** your business idea in three sentences or less and **Declare** how it will help others or provide a positive impact in the business community at large. There will be times when you will have to **Defend** your business idea to those who will call it impossible, unreasonable, and a waste of your time. However, you must **Determine** to possess all the knowledge regarding your business idea and its industry to become an expert in that field.

Excerpts taken from Dr. Ira V. Hilliard

Over time that knowledge will become wisdom and wisdom is what God promises to give you. Wisdom assists you in creating good plans, which allows you to possess whatever it is you go after thereby causing you to realize prosperity and success.

Good friend, take to heart what I'm telling you; collect my counsels and guard them with your life. Tune your ears to the world of wisdom; set your heart on a life of understanding. That's right – if you make insight your priority and won't take no for an answer, searching for it like a prospector panning for gold, like an adventure on a treasure hunt, believe me, before you know it Fear-of-God will be yours; you'll have come upon the knowledge of God. And here's why: God give out wisdom free, is plainspoken in knowledge and understanding. He's a rich mine of common sense for those who live well, a personal body-guard to the candid and sincere. He keeps his eye on all who live honestly, and pays special attention to his loyally committed ones. So now you can pick out what's true and fair, find all the good trials. Lady wisdom will be your close friend and brother knowledge your pleasant companion.

Proverbs 2:1-11 The Message

As you can see wisdom and knowledge are vital to making good plans. As your company grows, you will grow in wisdom, knowledge and understanding to make better plans for your company. That is why your plans will change. The more you know, the more you grow. The more your company grows, the more your plans change. Remember that if growth does not occur, your company will become stagnant and die. Prepare your plans, give them to God, and be willing to embrace change, get ready to grow, and expect to change your plans. Remember new level of growth, new plans! It is a never-ending process.

BIBLICAL REFERENCE:
Take good counsel and accept correction – that's the way to live wisely and well. We humans keep brainstorming options and plans, but God's purposes prevails.

Proverbs 19:20-21 The Message

PLANNING QUESTIONS:

1. Are you good at making plans in your personal or professional life? If not, get someone to help you write out your plans?

2. Are you a person who follows through on the plans you develop?

3. Do you determine what it will cost you to implement your plans or do you jump right into your projects?

4. Do you commit your plans to God or just go it alone?

5. Are you able to go with the flow when your plans change, or are you frustrated when your plans change?

WHAT IS FAILURE?

Failure doesn't mean – You are a failure
It means – You have not succeeded.

Failure doesn't mean – You accomplished nothing
It means – You have learned something

Failure doesn't mean – You've been disgraced
It means – You were willing to try

Failure doesn't mean – You don't have it
It means – You have to do something in a different way

Failure doesn't mean – You are inferior
It means – You are not perfect.

Failure doesn't mean – You've wasted your life
It means – You have a reason to start afresh

Failure doesn't mean – You should give up
It means – It will take a little longer

Failure doesn't mean – God has abandoned you
It means – God has a better way for you

"I can do ALL things through Christ which strengthens me."
Philippians 4:13 KJV

Unknown Author via E-Mail

NOTES

SPIRITUAL PRINCIPLE #5
Get Dressed For The Day (Before you go outside, put your makeup on and make sure you are wearing two suits)

> *Since you've got to 'put on a happy face',*
> *You might as well use Jesus as your foundation (makeup)!*
> **Carla A. Nelson**

WHAT'S UNDER YOUR GROUND?

BIBLICAL REFERENCE:
Whosoever cometh to me, and heareth my sayings, and doeth them, I will show you to whom he is like: He is like a man which built an house, and digged deep, and laid the foundation on a rock: and when the flood arose, the stream beat vehemently upon that house, and could not shake it: for it was founded upon a rock. But he that heareth, and doeth not, is like a man that without a foundation built an house upon the earth; against which the stream did beat vehemently, and immediately it fell; and the ruin of that house was great.
Luke 6:47-49 KJV

Throughout the four gospels Jesus refers to the kingdom of God in agricultural terms. In Luke 15:1-5, Jesus states:

▼ God is the ***husbandman*** - the farmer. He purges the branches to produce more fruit so He can have a plenteous harvest.

▼ Jesus is the ***true vine*** - the climbing flexible stem of a plant. The supplier of life where nourishment flows to the branches.

▼ We are the ***branches*** - a secondary stem growing from the main vine of a plant. A branch is also a part of a business organization or to extend or diversify as in one's business interests.

I am the true vine, and my Father is the husbandman. Every branch in me that beareth not fruit he taketh away: and every branch that beareth fruit, he purgeth it, that it may bring forth more fruit. Now ye are clean through the word which I have spoken unto you. Abide in me, and I in you. As the branch

cannot bear fruit of itself, except it abide in the vine; no more can ye, except ye abide in me. I am the vine, ye are the branches: He that abideth in me, and I in him, the same bringeth forth much fruit: for without me ye can do nothing.
1 John 15:1-5 KJV

It is the branches that bear the fruit for others to eat and be nourished. You are the branch (your business idea) that produces fruit (your product or service) to supply the nourishment (meeting the needs) of others. The growth and quality of your fruit (product or service) will be based on the quality of your soil (the condition of your heart). The deeper your roots in the soil (your understanding and application of God's word in your heart) will determine how well your plant handles tough situations.

My question to you is, *what's under your ground*? How deep are your roots in that ground? Being underground is to operate beneath the surface. It is something done in hiding or in secret, yet characterized by the work or action taking place underground. I remember doing an experiment in elementary school of planting a bean in a Styrofoam cup of soil, wait to see how long it would take to see the first green stem, and watch to see how long it would take to grow into a full-grown bean plant. Although it would take about a week or more to see the first green stem, that did not mean there was no work or action taking place underground, in secret, hiding from my eyes.

All plants grow down first before they grow up. So should it be with your business idea. To grow down is to do the necessary research and planning for the business idea (setting a sure foundation) before it can grow up and become a strong mature company to meet the needs of others.

As you grow and develop your company you will have many instances when you will have to put on a happy face when there is nothing to be happy about. There will be days when you will ask yourself *'why in the world did I decide to start this company? Nothing is going the way I planned and it looks like I'm headed towards failure'*. Remember things are not always what they seem. That is why Jesus says that you are to abide in Him and He will abide in you, for without Him you can do nothing. When the situations of starting and growing your company   look their worst, realize you are just going through something called a STORM.

You see it is one thing to start and grow your company the way the world says you should; it is another thing to start and grow your company the way God told you. The world will suggest that you borrow against the equity of your home (if you have one), to take out a small business loan (if you have good credit), or withdrawal from your 401K or pension plan (if you have anything left based on this economy). It is altogether different when you dedicate your business idea to God from its inception and allow Him to lead you all the way.

There are plenty of business institutions, seminars, books and tapes that tell you how to start your business idea by borrowing money and getting into debt. One of the main reasons why the U.S. Small Business Administration exists is to guarantee your loan from the bank you borrowed it from for your business, but your credit, collateral, and character must be of a certain low ratio of risk before they will even consider you or your business plan. I have not found an institution, seminar, book or tape explaining how to start a business relying on God to give you everything you need (resources = wisdom, people, material resources, and money) to successfully develop and manage it. This is why keeping company with God is so important!

Relying on God through Jesus Christ to build and grow your company according to kingdom principles is like building upon a Rock. Relying on any other source to tell you what to do is like building your company upon the Sand. When the stormy conditions come, which foundation do you want your company built on, the Rock or the Sand?

The stormy conditions will come in the form of bad economic conditions. The river overflowing its banks will come in the form of having more bills and debt than revenue and income to pay them all on time, in time, or just before repossession time, if at all! But as with everything in life these conditions will come and pass.

Weather conditions are known as seasons and business conditions are known as cycles. Everyone who is in business for him/herself goes through it, so it is best to be properly prepared.

Build your business foundation strong in Jesus (the Rock) so you can endure the rough times and have something left when it is over. When the storm is over use what is left over and regroup. In the business world it is called reorganization. If you build your business foundation in the world's way (the Sand), when the storm is over you will be wiped out; in the business world it is called bankruptcy!

Having Jesus as your foundation will allow you to smile and put on a happy face during the stormy times of your business life because you know if He brought you to it He will bring you through it. Build your company on the word of God and use His word to get you through every situation you encounter good or bad. The Bible truly does have an answer to every problem you face. You just have to be diligent in finding the right passages, to understand and apply God's word in your heart. It's call tilling the soil! Therefore, build your company on a solid foundation – the Rock – Jesus Christ.

BIBLICAL REFERENCE:
These words I speak to you are not mere additions to your life, homeowner improvements to your standard of living. They are foundation words, words to build a life on. If you work the words into your life, you are like a smart carpenter who dug deep and laid the foundation of his house on bedrock. When the river burst its banks and crashed against the house, nothing could shake it; it was built to last. But if you use my words in Bible studies and don't work them into your life, you are like a dumb carpenter who built a house but skipped the foundation. When the swollen river came crashing in, it collapsed like a house of cards. It was a total loss.

Luke 6:47-49 The Message

WHAT'S UNDER YOUR GROUND QUESTIONS:

1. What kind of seed (product or service) do you intend on planting?

2. What kind of soil do you have? What is the condition of your heart to understand and apply God's word in your business idea?

3. Are you able to handle tough situations by applying God's word to the problem or circumstance you are facing?

4. Are you able to ride the storms in your life or do you find yourself sinking in the middle of the situation?

5. Are you building your business idea on the Rock of Jesus Christ or on sinking sand?

SPIRITUAL PRINCIPLE #5
Get Dress For The Day (Before you go outside, put your makeup on and make sure you are wearing two suits)

When putting on your best suit for that important business meeting,
Don't forget your Armor!

Carla A. Nelson

APPEARANCE MATTERS

BIBLICAL REFERENCE:
... be strong in the Lord, and in the power of his might. Put on the whole armour of God, that ye may be able to stand against the wiles of the devil. For we wrestle not against flesh and blood, but against principalities, against powers, against the rulers of the darkness of this world, against spiritual wickedness in high places. Wherefore take unto you the whole armour of God, that ye may be able to withstand in the evil day, and having done all, to stand. Stand therefore, having your loins girt about with truth, and having on the breastplate of righteousness; And your feet shod with the preparation of the gospel of peace; Above all, taking the shield of faith, wherewith ye shall be able to quench all the fiery darts of the wicked. And take the helmet of salvation, and the sword of the Spirit, which is the word of God: Praying always with all prayer and supplication in the Spirit, and watching thereunto with all persever-ance and supplication for all saints.

Ephesians 6:10-18 KJV

As a citizen of the kingdom of God you live in two worlds, the physical and the spiritual. Therefore, when you get dress for work, you need to put on two suits. Your physical clothes to cover your physical body as you go out into the world and do business, and your spiritual clothes cover your spiritual body to protect the real you from the enemy as you do business.

Your physical clothes should be one of quality. It is important to look your best when you conduct your business affair with the world. People pass judgement on you based on first impressions, and that first impression is usually made by what you have on. As a kingdom citizen you are a representation of God's best, you are God's example to the world of what He provides for those who live for Him.

For the man:

▼ *Your face, hair and nails should be neatly groomed and clean.*

▼ *Your shirt should be clean and pressed.*

▼ *Your tie should be straight.*

▼ *Your suit should fit you properly and be pressed, cleaned; no missing buttons.*

▼ *Your shoes shined and no cracks on the sides or holes in the sole!*

▼ *Your cologne should not be overpowering or offensive!*

For the woman:

▼ *Your hair should be combed and in place.*

▼ *Your make up should be clean and understated.*

▼ *Your dress or skirt at a proper length (the mini length has no place in the kingdom or in business, but that is another book).*

▼ *Your pantyhose should not have runs in them or sag at the ankles.*

▼ *Your shoes should be neat and no run over heels!*

▼ *Your perfume should not be overpowering or offensive!*

Your spiritual clothes are the full armor of God that is listed in Ephesians 6:11-18. These verses are often misinterpreted to state that you are to do battle *with* the enemy. Verse 12 indicates that you do not wrestle against flesh and blood but against principalities, powers, rulers of the darkness of this world and against spiritual wickedness in high places. You are to dress for protection from the enemy (satan).

▼ *Your loins girt about with truth* - *the loins are where your emotions and reproduction reside both naturally and spiritually.*

▼ *Your breastplate of righteousness* - *to be in the right position with God is a matter of the heart.*

▼ *Your feet shod with the preparation of the gospel of peace* - *you are a representative of the kingdom of God no matter where you go.*

▼ *Your shield of faith, wherewith you shall be able to quench all the fiery darts of the wicked* - *your faith in God protects you from the enemy and his shrapnel of fear.*

▼ *Your helmet of salvation* - *you have the mind of Christ and the wisdom and knowledge of God.*

▼ *Your sword of the Spirit, which is the word of God* - *knowing and saying God's word is how you beat the enemy at his game.*

While your physical body is going about the day conducting business with the world, your spiritual body is standing at attention fully protecting you from the evils of the world.

Notice, I did not say that you are to get dressed to do battle *with* the enemy. *To engage in combat or controversy, to contend with full strength* is to do battle with the devil, this is not what God wants you to do. In II Chronicles 20:15, Jahaziel told Johosaphat that the battle was not his but God's. In Ephesians 6:13, Paul tells the saints at Ephesus to withstand during the evil day and verse 16, states that your shield of faith will quench the fiery darts of the wicked. Nowhere in the Bible does it state that YOU are to fight. You are to STAND, PRAY, and go get the REWARD that God has for you after the battle is over.

> *If you are having problems standing, you are probably improperly dressed!*
> **Dr. Charles Phillips**

Now to fight the good fight of faith or fight for what is yours it is another thing. To *Fight* is to *strive to overcome, struggle to endure, or to manage in an unnecessarily rough or awkward manner.* You must keep watch over your company. The survival of it is based on how diligent you are in overseeing the growth and development of your business idea. There will be days, weeks, months, and sometimes years when you will have to endure and fight for your vision. You will find yourself like Nehemiah, keeping a weapon in your hand while managing your company with the other. You must be vigilant and prepared to fight the battle to keep your business idea alive.

And it came to pass, when our enemies heard that it was known unto us, and God had brought their counsel to nought, that we returned all of us to the wall, every one unto his work. And it came to pass from that time forth, that the half of my servants wrought in the work, and the other half of them held both the spears, the shields, and the bows, and the habergeons, and the rulers were behind all the house of Judah. They which builded on the wall, and they bare burdens, with those that laded, every one with one of his hands wrought in the work, and with the other hand held a weapon. For the builders, every one had his sword girded by his side, and so builded. And he that sounded the trumpet was by me.

Nehemiah 4:15-18 KJV

When you feel the emotional strains, the financial obstacles, and the operational pressures of your company, know that it is the enemy trying to beat you up and wear you down. You will wonder why all of these negative circumstances (the circles you stand in) are happening to you. It seems like no matter how much you try to overcome them (step out of the negative circle), satan has another one ready for you to step into. Know that it is not so much YOU that he's after, but God's purpose and mandate that are to be done in the earth through YOU. The enemy will do whatever he has to do to kill, steal and destroy you and your vision.

The enemy is also after your faith. If you do not have the faith to endure and see your vision manifest, you will begin to fear and doubt that it will ever happen. The devil responds to your fear just like God responds to your faith. He will always come to wear you down when you are weak and where you are doubtful. He waits until you are not at your best, or something you were working on does not turn out the way you wanted it to and screams fear and doubt into your heart. It is your responsibility to scream back at him the word of God and remind him that you are a citizen of the Kingdom of God. *No weapon that is formed against thee (me) shall prosper; and every tongue that shall rise against thee (me) in judgment thou (I) shalt condemn...* (Isaiah 54:17a KJV). This is how you fight. Saying this verse of scripture out loud is what my Pastor calls hitting satan where it hurts him the most. He hates to hear the word of God coming out of our mouth (this is another reason to say your prayers aloud).

If satan is going to use words of doubt to kill your vision, then you need to use God's word to shut him up and make him flee! That is your weapon! This is why it is vital that you study the Bible. When you are in a fight, you do not have time to go find a scripture to beat him up with. You need to know the scriptures and have them planted in your heart. That way the next time he tries to tell you that your business idea won't work or that your company is going to fail, you can stop him in the middle of his sentence with the word of God and tell him a scripture or two! If you are going to give him a *'piece of your mind'*, it might as well be the mind of Christ!

In Matthew 4:1-11, we read where Jesus took a 40-day fast right after he was baptized. Let us consider that the beginning of his company. Here is where we see satan confronting Jesus because he was watching during His fast and realized Jesus was physically weak. We read how satan began to tempt Jesus with the same three things we are tempted with in life, ***appetites, fame, and power***. Let's look at how Jesus handled satan with his fast and compare it to how we should handle our business while laying the foundation for our company.

1st Temptation – PROVISIONS – Appetites (verses 2-3)
God has not given me what I need when I think or feel I need it.

JESUS	He was hungry and without strength.(The human body cannot go without water more than 40 days).
BUSINESS	You have a lack of resources. (The company cannot survive without sufficient resources.)

Do you want to wait for God to feed you (provide for you), or do you want to do it with your own will? If God doesn't give you what you think you need, it may be that you should not have it, you don't need it, or it is not the time for you to have it!

Jesus said that man must not live by bread alone but by every word that proceeds out of the mouth of God. Read God's word in the Bible to find out how to obtain your recourses. God is your true and original source!

2nd Temptation EXPECTING GOD TO PERFORM – Fame
(verses 5-7)
God does not always give us what we want when we want it.

JESUS	Showed patience by enduring hard times knowing that God is in control. Jesus knew His position in the kingdom and was not anxious for instant notoriety.
BUSINESS	You make an error in judgment trying to get rich or famous quickly, only to find yourself asking God to get you out of the mess you made.

Having a successful company takes time and patience. You don't want to have *'15 minutes of fame'*, and an lifetime of misery trying to keep the company profitable. God does not automatically make you an instant success, or answer you right away when you ask Him to get you out of your mess, especially when you did not seek His counsel before you made an unwise decision. Sometimes God will leave you alone with just His word to see how you will handle the situation.

3rd Temptation - QUESTION THE PLAN OF GOD - Power
(verses 8-10)
God does not show me an entire roadmap to success.

JESUS	satan wanted Jesus to submit and worship him with the promise to give Jesus power and authority over the world.
BUSINESS	We want wealth, success, and power, and we want it NOW. We will look for the short cuts to get the next level quickly without the struggle; not realizing that

it is in the struggle that we learn to handle the pressures at the next level.

Jesus said we are to worship and serve God Only. Seek yea first the Kingdom of God and all things (including power) will be added unto you. God does not need satan to tell you where you need to go or what you need to do. It is a trap. Don't believe people who tell you *'it does not take all of that'* to have a successful company, or *'you can become an instant millionaire in 30 days"*!

Don't put God to the test or back him up in a corner to perform a miracle for you. You must read the scriptures for yourself daily seeking God's council for wisdom and guidance in your daily affairs. He will provide you with the answers you need when you need them. That is what keeping company with God is about.

> *Your greatest temptation will always come at your weakest moment in life.*
> *It is then we should run to God, not run from Him.*
>
> **Carla A. Nelson**

When you overcome temptations you defeat satan. It is at this time that the angels assigned to you will minister to you as they did Jesus in verse 11. Your angels will:

▼ *Bless You:*
For the Son of man shall come in the glory of his Father with his angels; and then he shall reward every man according to his works.
Matthew 16:27 KJV

▼ *Comfort You*
Seeing it is a righteous thing with God to recompense tribulation to them that trouble you; And to you who are troubled rest with us, when the Lord Jesus shall be revealed from heaven with his mighty angels,
2 Thessalonians 1:6-7 KJV

▼ *Encourage You*
Bless the LORD, ye his angels, that excel in strength, that do his commandments, hearkening unto the voice of his word. Bless ye the LORD, all ye his hosts; ye ministers of his, that do his pleasure.
Psalm 103:20-21

▼ Deliver You

This poor man cried, and the LORD heard him, and saved him out of all his troubles. The angel of the LORD encampeth round about them that fear him, and delivereth them. O taste and see that the LORD is good: blessed is the man that trusteth in him.

Psalm 34:6-8 KJV

Then Nebuchadnezzar spake, and said, Blessed be the God of Shadrach, Meshach, and Abednego, who hath sent his angel, and delivered his servants that trusted in him, and have changed the king's word, and yielded their bodies, that they might not serve nor worship any god, except their own God.

Daniel 3:28 KJV

▼ Feed You

But he himself went a day's journey into the wilderness, and came and sat down under a juniper tree: and he requested for himself that he might die; and said, It is enough; now, O LORD, take away my life; for I am not better than my fathers. And as he lay and slept under a juniper tree, behold, then an angel touched him, and said unto him, Arise and eat. And he looked, and, behold, there was a cake baken on the coals, and a cruse of water at his head. And he did eat and drink, and laid him down again. And the angel of the LORD came again the second time, and touched him, and said, Arise and eat; because the journey is too great for thee. And he arose, and did eat and drink, and went in the strength of that meat forty days and forty nights unto Horeb the mount of God.

1 Kings 19:4-8 KJV

▼ Protect You

For he shall give his angels charge over thee, to keep thee in all thy ways. They shall bear thee up in their hands, lest thou dash thy foot against a stone.

Psalm 91:11-12 KJV

Thinkest thou that I cannot now pray to my Father, and he shall presently give me more than twelve legions of angels?

Matthew 26:53 KJV

Remember that you have a guardian angel and a legion of angels (6,000) assigned to fight for you and protect you from all manner of evil. It is your angels that bring forth the answers to your prayers from the spiritual to the natural realm. When you audibly pray to

God, remind Him of His word and promises to you. Your prayer puts your angels on assignment. If you do not see any activity towards the process of your vision it could be that your angels are sitting, listening and waiting to hear from you!

BIBLICAL REFERENCE:

…God is strong, and he wants you strong, so take everything the Master has set out for you, well-made weapons of the best materials. And put them to use so you will be able to stand up to everything the devil throws your way. This is no afternoon athletic contest that we'll walk away from and forget about in a couple of hours. This is for keeps, a life-or-death fight to the finish against the devil and all his angels. Be prepared. You're up against far more than you can handle on your own. Take all the help you can get, every weapon God has issued, so that when it's all over but the shouting you'll still be on your feet. Truth, righteousness, peace, faith, and salvation are more than words. Learn how to apply them. You'll need them throughout your life. God's Word is an indispensable weapon. In the same way, prayer is essential in this ongoing warfare. Pray hard and long. Pray for your brothers and sisters. Keep each other's spirits up so that no one falls behind or drops out.

Ephesians 6:10-18 The Message

GET DRESSED FOR THE DAY QUESTIONS:

1. Are you a person that is able to endure adversity?

2. Are you a person that gives up on a project when it looks like it will fail or do you continue until the project is over?

3. Are you diligent about studying the scriptures for yourself or do you believe and/or quote what other people say is in the Bible?

4. Do you have a 'good suit' with the proper accessories you can wear when conducting your business affairs or meeting your clients?

5. Is your physical appearance acceptable or do you need to make an appointment to have your hair, nails, and feet properly groomed?

6. Is your spiritual armor clean, shinny, strong and reinforced?

7. Do you fight your own battles or do you allow God to do it for you?

8. Are you willing to speak God's word over your life so you can activate your angels?

The Other Ten Commandments

1. Thou shall not worry, for worry is the unproductive of all human activities.

2. Thou shall not be fearful, for most of the things we fear never come to pass.

3. Thou shall not cross bridges before you come to them, for no one yet has succeeded in accomplishing this.

4. Thou shall face each problem as it comes. You can only handle one at a time anyway.

5. Thou shall not take problems to bed with you, for they make very poor bedfellows.

6. Thou shall not borrow other people's problems. They can better care for them than you can.

7. Thou shall not try to relive yesterday for good or ill, it is forever gone. Concentrate on what is happening in your life and be happy now!

8. Thou shall be a good listener, for only when you listen do you hear different ideas from your own. It is hard to learn something new when you are talking, and some people do know more than you do.

9. Thou shall not become "bogged down" by frustration, for ninety percent of it is rooted in self-pity and will only interfere with positive action.

10. BONUS: Thou shall count thy blessings, never overlooking the small ones, for a lot of small blessings add up to a big one.

Author Unknown via E-Mail

NOTES

SPIRITUAL PRINCIPLE #6
Counting The Cost (Are you able and capable of operating your own company?)

> *Going into business requires certain personal characteristics,*
> *experience and skills.*
> *Managing a company is like seeing a Lion in the zoo;*
> *the fence safeguards you.*
> *Owning a company is like seeing a Lion in the Jungle with nowhere to run!*
> *Carla A. Nelson*

YOUR PERSONAL LIFE
Necessary Considerations Before Pursing Your Business Idea

BIBLICAL REFERENCE:
Go to the ant, thou sluggard; consider her ways, and be wise: Which having no guide, overseer, or ruler, Provideth her meat in the summer, and gathereth her food in the harvest. How long wilt thou sleep, O sluggard? when wilt thou arise out of thy sleep? Yet a little sleep, a little slumber, a little folding of the hands to sleep: So shall thy poverty come as one that travelleth, and thy want as an armed man.

Proverbs 6:6-11 KJV

Your Personal Life will be affected in every way, so get ready for CHANGE! There are **Four** major aspects of your personal life you need to consider when starting your business, especially if you are going to do it on a full time basis.

1. *The Initial Investment*
2. *Calculating Business Income*
3. *Your Support System*
4. *Spiritual and Social Communities*

This is not the time to take it easy or be lazy. This is the time to determine if you really have what it takes to start your business idea and build it into a profitable company.

Some people start their business with money from their savings or investments (401k, mutual or money market accounts, stocks, bonds, etc.) Others will borrow against the equity of their home or other real estate, and then there are those of you who will pay for it as you go with whatever extra money you have left from your paycheck (and sacrifice going out to eat every weekend), to purchase items for your business idea.

Most of you will need additional cash to continue operations until that first sale is made, the contract you were working on comes through, or your business loan is approved. That is where borrowing from friends and family come into the picture. These are the friends and family members who said your vision to start this business was a good idea, it must have come from God, or validated the need for it in the market place. These are the people who said they would assist you with anything you needed to get the business off the ground, or would be there for you no matter what!

Now is the time to put their words to the test. Now is the time to find out where their commitment is with you and your vision. As you calculate the initial monetary investment for the business (called the *Initial Capital Requirement in the business plan in Spiritual Principle #7*), answer the following:

1. THE INITIAL INVESTMENT
Money
    a. How much money do you presently have?
    b. Determine the amount of your own money you are willing to put into the company.
    c. Are you willing to invest ALL of your savings, stocks and bonds into your business idea?
    d. Have you calculated how much money (realistic) you can live off of for personal needs and expenses?
    e. Determine how much of your own money you are willing to donate to support the company before you bail out, (because you realized the vision to start a business was not from God). What is the time period you will allow before this decision is made?

f. Document in writing if you are GIVING this money to the company or if it is a loan. If it is a loan, specify when the company plans to pay it back.

g. Determine how much money you will need to borrow through investors, lines of credit, financial entities, or loans from your friends or family members.

h. If someone else (a friend or family member) is giving you money towards the company, repeat letter **f**.

Equipment, Furniture and Supplies

Since the company has not earned any money, anything you purchase will be out of your own pocket.

a. Determine what kind of equipment you need to get started. (Fax, copier, printer, computer)

b. Indicate the furniture that will be used in the name of the company (especially if it is a home based business).

c. Keep receipts of all materials and supplies purchased for company use. Keep accurate records of mileage used for business meetings, appointments, and travel.

d. Document in writing and save receipts of all these purchases. They will be needed for your personal and business taxes as well as become a part of your corporate papers should you decide to incorporate the company.

Location, Vehicles, and other Real Property

You may be in a position where you own (free and clear) real property or take the equity out of your home to use for the initial investment of the company. A document or transfer of title should be prepared for each piece of property indicating that it will be used for business purposes. This will be needed for your personal and business taxes as well as become a part of your corporate papers should you decide to incorporate the company.

When I counseled new entrepreneurs at the U.S Small Business Administration Small Business Development Center, working on their business plan, many of them found it difficult to project the amount of money they would realistically plan to make in their first year of business. They had an idea how much money they wanted to make, but they did not know how to calculate the cost of doing business, especially when calculating operational and intangible expenses. We will discuss this in more detail in *Obtaining Office Space in Spiritual Principle #7*. As you calculate the amount of money you want the business to make, don't forget to calculate how much it cost to operate the business. Here are some points to consider:

2. CALCULATING BUSINESS INCOME

    a. Can the business support your personal and business needs? If not now, when (give a specific time)?

    b. How much money will you need to keep your company operating with a positive cash flow?

    c. Do you have a guaranteed source of income/client base?

    d. Have you found reliable vendors to assist you when you start your company?

    e. When stating (in writing) how much you want to make in a given time period, indicate if it is your *gross* or *net* profit.

    f. How much money do you plan to make during your first, second, third, fourth, and fifth year of your business?

    g. Do you plan to measure your increases in terms of dollars or percentages?

To realize how much you have to make in order to receive a profit, use the following formula:

Break Even Analysis:
    <u>Required Data:</u>
    1. Average Selling Price per unit of <u>Product</u> or <u>Service</u>
    2. Average Direct cost per unit of <u>Product</u> or <u>Service</u>
    3. Total Estimated Fixed and Overhead Expenses

Calculations:
1. Contribution Margin = Sales Price/Unit – Variable Cost/Unit
2. Gross Profit % = Gross Profit/Unit ÷ Selling Price/Unit
3. Break Even Point (Units) = Fixed Expenses ÷ Contribution Margin
4. Break Even Point (Sales Dollars) = Fixed Expenses ÷ Average Gross Profit %

Hours Of Operation

When you start your company there will be many trade offs. One of them is the 9:00 a.m. to 5:00 p.m. daily grind to a job that does not relate to your vision. The flip side to that is you may have to work a 7:00 a.m. to 8:00 p.m. workday, but what makes it bearable is that you will be following your vision and fulfilling the mandate God gave you (your purpose in life). When determining what your hours of operation will be you will need to:

1. Determine how much time are you going to work at your business?
2. Decide if you plan to start it on a part time basis or full time basis?

▼ *Part Time*
- How many days in the week and how many hours in the day?
- What is the length of time you will give yourself before you decide to work the business full time and make it your sole source of income?

▼ *Full Time*
- What are the days in the week and the hours of the day?
- Which days is the business closed? (Even if it is home based)

▼ *Home Based Businesses*
It is important to know that you must set aside time in your day that you will only do the work of the company and not the work of the household on company time. This will help discipline you in your work habits and set the standard for the policy and procedures of your company.

3. YOUR SUPPORT SYSTEM

You will need to have a conversation with those persons within your *Circle of Influence* to let them know what you are about to do. Obtaining their support, encouragement and possibly their financial contribution is critical to the success of your business idea. Your *circle of influence* at minimum are your

▼ *Spouse*
▼ *Child(ren)*
▼ *Parent(s)*
▼ *Other Family Member(s)*
▼ *Close Friend(s) or Partner in the business*

Your Circle of Influence

Prepare a mini business plan (*see the section Basic Essentials For A Winning Business Plan in Spiritual Principle #7 Business Fundamentals*), to discuss with your circle of influence about the nature of your business idea and how the vision came to you. After you discuss with them your business idea, you need to find out the following information from them:

▼ What is their initial reaction (verbal and non-verbal communication) when you told them you heard from God and plan to start your own company?

▼ What is the level of support you expect to receive from them, if any?

▼ Are they willing to *ride the tide* with you? If so, how far out (of their way) are they willing to go?

▼ What are their concerns and how were you able to answer their questions with the plans you have written for the business idea?

▼ Have you properly communicated to them and do they fully understand and comprehend how much time you will have to allocate to the company?

▼ As time goes on, will it require more of your time?

▼ Do you need their help in *any* way? If yes, have you communicated exactly what you need from them (time, talent, tender)?

> Tender - *An unconditional offer of money or service in satisfaction of debt or obligation made to save a penalty or forfeiture for nonpayment or nonperformance. An offer or proposal for acceptance as or an offer of a bid for a contract. Something that may be offered in payment.*

▼ Which Light are they giving you?

> **Green light** - to move forward. It is a good idea and it is about time you did something about it.
>
> **Yellow light** - to caution you. Slow down on the timetable, do some more research, or re-count your costs.
>
> **Red light** - to stop you. You have missed a critical step in planning such as you are in debt way over your head, you want to immediately quit your full time job with no immediate income to live on. Or you have missed God because you do not have the talent, skills intellect or ability to do what you want to do.

Your *circle of influence* is your first point to test the marketability of your business idea because they know you best. This is not to say that if they don't agree with you, you should not go forward. What I am saying is these people are constantly in your life and they know if you have what it takes (the characteristics) to stick with it and make it happen.

Health and Fitness

Keeping yourself physically and emotionally fit is a vital component to starting your company. If you, the one who envisioned this business idea, are not healthy, how do you expect it to manifest into a successful company? You might know that the body is the temple of the Lord but did you know that your body shelters the mind, which is where the vision resides? If the body is weak or ill, the mind does not receive the proper nutrition to function. A weak or ill mind will produce a weak or ill-fated company. Therefore, when making plans and setting the standards for your company, include plans and standards for your body:

▼ *Eat healthy foods and eat at the right time of day (breakfast, lunch and dinner).*
▼ *Exercise regularly and structure it for the same time of the day at least three times a week.*
▼ *Exhale from the stress of the day and take time for yourself at least a half- day, once a week.*
▼ *Ease yourself into your quiet time at night and get proper rest on a daily basis.*

4. SPIRITUAL AND SOCIAL COMMUNITIES

Your *spiritual and social communities* are the next places to test the marketability of your business idea. You share common values, create bonds, and have open and honest communications with the people you fellowship with on a consistent basis. If you test market your product or service to the following groups, you may have a good indication of the demand for your product or service and if any modifications are necessary.

Spiritually

Worship and fellowship with God is the most intimate time of your life. If you are truly a citizen of the kingdom of God you should be able to discuss your business idea with your spiritual authority (Pastor, Rabbi, Minister, or Priest) and ask him or her to bless it.

These people are a good source of inspiration and motivation. When times get tough (and they will) it is a comforting thought to know your spiritual authority can assist you with your endeavors through prayer, agreement, and encouragement, as well as provide you connections or referrals to people that have the resources you need (provision).

They will also tell you if your business idea does not line up with kingdom principles. If your business idea causes you to miss all Sabbath worship times, then it is probably not the right business for you to pursue. Here are some obvious examples of what I mean:

▼ *A Christian owning a liquor store, selling lottery tickets, or managing an off-track betting company.*

▼ *A Moslem owning a meat market selling pork and catfish.*

▼ *A Hebrew operating their business on a Friday after dusk or Saturday.*

▼ *A Catholic operating a plan parenthood agency or an abortion clinic.*

I would hope that God, Jesus Christ, Holy Spirit, or your Circle of Influence gives you the **Red Light** before you take a foolish idea like these to your spiritual authority for a blessing!

Social
The fraternal, sorority, humanitarian, or community organization you belong to provide a great place to start selling your business idea. These people will tell you:

▼ *What areas of your business they like or dislike as a customer or a supplier?*

▼ *What other people have tried to do in their company that worked or did not work, and why?*

▼ *What you can do to improve your business idea?*

▼ *If they will buy from you again; why or why not; and most of all...*

▼ *Will they tell others to buy from you? This is called a referral – this will be the true test of a good business idea!*

Don't be alarmed by the answers you receive from conducting these surveys. It is better to find out if your vision is a moneymaking venture or not before you pour your life savings into it. Don't be offended if those you considered your friends and family members do not support your business idea. Everyone cannot go where you are going, so learn to love them and leave them where they are. As you keep company with God, you will find no better friend than Him!

BIBLICAL REFERENCE:
You lazy fool, look at an ant. Watch it closely: let it teach you a thing or two. Nobody has to tell it what to do. All summer it stores up food; at harvest it stockpiles provisions. So how long are you going to laze around doing nothing? How long before you get out of bed? A nap here, a nap there, a day off here, a day off there, sit back, take it easy – do you know what comes next? Just this: You can look forward to a dirt-poor life, poverty your permanent houseguest!
Proverbs 6:6-11 The Message

YOUR PERSONAL LIFE QUESTIONS:
In your Personal or Professional Life

	YES	NO	NOT SURE
1. Do you properly budget your personal finances?	____	____	____
2. Do you properly budget your professional finances?	____	____	____
3. Do you properly manage your business time?	____	____	____
4. Are you able to work 12-16 hours a day?	____	____	____
5. Are you pleasant, courteous yet firm with your customers even when they are rude to you?	____	____	____
6. Are you able to set aside personal time for yourself on a weekly basis?	____	____	____
7. Are you willing to spend quality spiritual time on a daily basis?	____	____	____
8. Are you able to handle constructive criticism?	____	____	____
9. Are you a leader?	____	____	____
10. Do you enjoy competition?	____	____	____

SPIRITUAL PRINCIPLE #6
Counting The Cost (Are you able and capable of operating your own company?)

> *You should always surround yourself with key people who will play a*
> *Crucial role in the structure of your company.*
> *You Can't Start One Without Them!*
>
> **Carla A. Nelson**

The RED TEAM

BIBLICAL REFERENCE:
Without counsel purposes are disappointed: but in the multitude of counsellors they are established.

Proverbs 15:22 KJV

For most of your life you have been told that before you make a critical or life changing decision, it is wise to talk to your parents, teachers, spiritual authorities or counselors. These people had the wisdom and experience you needed to help you make life or death decisions about your life, career, spirituality, or social involvement.

I call my business team my *Red Team* because I am a 1960's child and grew up watching Batman and Robin. Whenever the Commissioner was in trouble and needed a case solved that no one could solve, he would pick up the Red Phone that was a direct line to Bruce Wayne (Batman). No matter where he was, Bruce Wayne would stop what he was doing and come to the rescue. The people who are on your team should be like Batman, ready and willing to work with you because they believe in you and they realize that your vision can become a successful company. These people are not necessarily persons you would have on your Board of Directors (if you need one). They are people who have your best interest at heart! The Red Team are people who:

▼ *Can assist you in making key decisions in your company. They know a good opportunity when the see one.*

▼ *You can call on at a moment's notice and talk to them about a concern or issue regarding your company.*

▼ *Know the importance of Image. They know how to make you look good!*

▼ *Know how to get you out of a bad situation and work things out for you.*

▼ *Can give you encouragement and motivate you when you are not at your best.*

▼ *Know when to push, prod, provoke, promote and praise you.*

▼ *Know when and how to tell you YES, NO or WAIT!*

1. *Attorney* - one who concentrates in the field of business law. Particularly in the field of small business, corporate or contract law.

2. *Accountant* - one who is an expert in business accounting and tax laws. Preferably a Certified Public Accountant (CPA).

3. *Banker* - one who works at the local branch or works in the small business banking division. When you need special banking services, they can get it done for you.

4. *Business Coach* - one who is probably your mentor. They know what is important to you personally and professionally and can hold your hand through your spiritual storms.

5. *Financial Consultant* - one who can advise you on how to allocate, save, invest and spend your money. They keep you informed on market trends, how to save for a rainy day, create a

financial portfolio for you, and invest your future earnings for you and the company.

6. *Insurance Broker* - one who informs you of the types of insurance needed for the type of business you want to start. All insurance companies do not cover all types of businesses. It is important to know if your company can cover all of their insurance needs.

7. *Public Relations Consultant* - one who understands you and your market. They know what publications are suitable to promote your business, they write articles about your business or arrange for interviews, they know where best to market your goods and services, and where you need to be to promote yourself!

8. *Spiritual Authority* - (Pastor, Rabbi, Minister, or Priest). He/She is a good source of inspiration and motivation. They believe in what you want to do and are able to minister to you concerning your vision. They can comfort, discipline, encourage, and guide you in with kingdom principles and wisdom. *(Discussed in more detail in the section Your Personal Life – Spiritually in Spiritual Principle #6.)*

It is vital to your company to have a good relationship with your accountant, attorney, banker and your spiritual authority at minimum. Every successful business owner values (and sometimes relies on) the wisdom they have and the advice they give, sometimes on a daily basis. If you are going to rely on someone that much, it is vital to have a good working relationship with these people so take your time selecting who you want on your team! *(See Business Coaches in the section "Where To Go For More Information" in References).*

BIBLICAL REFERENCE:
Refuse good advice and watch your plans fails; take good counsel and watch them succeed.

Proverbs 15:22 The Message

SPIRITUAL PRINCIPLE #6
Counting The Cost (Are you able and capable of operating your own company?)

> *Always make the deal at the table and*
> *Negotiate from a position of strength.*
>
> Moshe I. Powers

OBTAINING OFFICE SPACE

BIBLICAL REFERENCE:
Except the LORD build the house, they labour in vain that build it: except the LORD keep the city, the watchman waketh but in vain. It is vain for you to rise up early, to sit up late, to eat the bread of sorrows: for so he giveth his beloved sleep.

Psalm 127:1-2 KJV

One of the first things a new entrepreneur wants to do to validate his decision of starting a business is to obtain office space that is located outside of his residence. As with the information I shared with you in the previous chapter, you must first count the cost of having an outside office to determine if you can afford it. You should also pray and seek God to see if the timing is right to take on this added expense.

There is much to consider when deciding if office space is necessary for your company. Your business concept may be one that will work out well in the home, but there are others that must be done in an outside location because of the type of business it is. Businesses such as restaurants, hair and nail salons, retail boutiques, and auto repair shops are just a few types of companies that have to abide by State and Federal laws that may prohibit you from conducting business in the home.

Obtaining office space might be easy to do, but *maintaining* it is nothing less than an added burden. When there is no income coming in for the next sixty to ninety days, realize that the lease and utilities must be paid *every* thirty days. Office space and utilities are two large expenses that will cause your cash flow or reserves accounts to quickly depreciate to zero! One of the first things you must do is make sure you have at least 6-8 months of lease and utility costs (part of your operating expenses) in an account before you sign the lease papers.

If you are not sure where you want to be located or how much space you need, find a good commercial real estate broker to assist you. Usually their services are no cost to you because the person or company that is leasing or selling the space pays them. If he or she is not willing to assist you or if they are impatient with you, find another one! Ask someone you know that leases office space for a referral of a good commercial real estate broker. With this in mind I have listed eight components to consider before you purchase or lease office space.

1. Find a place or places you are interested in (Concept Design).
   - ▼ Home base: set aside a room specifically designated for your company
   - ▼ Office Space: multiplex office building
   - ▼ Virtual: business address for the mobile professional "at home" company

> *NOTE: All office space must meet certain code compliances regardless of its location.*

2. Determine the type of environment you want your company to be located.
   - ▼ Retail
   - ▼ Industrial
   - ▼ Professional
   - ▼ Medical
   - ▼ Mixture
   - ▼ Incubator
   - ▼ Inner City or Suburbs
   - ▼ HUD Zone

NOTE: Consider incentives from the leasing company, tax credits or employee incentives offered by the government for that location.

3. **Find out what amenities the location provides:**
   ▼ Access to major road arteries (major routes and highway arteries)
   ▼ Access to Metro & public transportation
   ▼ Security of area during the day and/or night
   ▼ Places to eat
   ▼ Shopping Centers
   ▼ Number of miles to your vendors & customers

4. **Find out what the city/county plans are for improvement in the area you are interested in.**
   ▼ What are the safety conditions in the area
   ▼ Development of Roads
   ▼ New Building Development
   ▼ Change from Residential to Commercially zoned property
   ▼ Tearing down of surround building
   ▼ Who owns the property and if they plan to sell it any time soon

5. **Call local utilities to find out what the average costs are for the year.**
   ▼ Electric or Gas
   ▼ Water (usually paid for by the property owner)
   ▼ Liability insurance for the office space
   ▼ Security (monitoring) system
   ▼ Is the building wired for Cable, DLS or Satellite T.V. lines
   ▼ How many telephone lines are available (connected to the building)

6. **Once you have found an office space/building you are interested in, find out:**
   ▼ What is the cost per square footage?
   ▼ What is included in the operating expense?
   ▼ How much is the operating expense per month?
   ▼ Can you sub-lease some of your space to another company or individual?
   ▼ What are the restrictions - find out what you can and cannot do in, on and around the property?
   ▼ Is any plumbing, electrical, phone, cabling work or wiring that needs to be done?
   ▼ Can you receive calls from your wireless phone in that area?
   ▼ Who are your neighbors in the office complex?

7. **Signing the Lease - understanding what your rights and responsibilities are BEFORE you sign:**
   ▼ Get advice from someone who's been through this process before and have them review the contract with you. (Use your Red Team).
   ▼ Know the financial and legal responsibilities before and during the renovation of your office space (if needed).
   ▼ Identify your financial operating costs for the office space on a monthly basis.
   ▼ Know what legal obligations you will incur should you decide or need to break the lease.

8. **Operating Cost:**

▼ *Rent*	$10 - $30 per square foot depending upon location
▼ *Electric*	$20-$30 per square foot of space per month
▼ *Phone*	Local, Toll & Long Distance calls 10¢ per outgoing call Basic monthly charge per line Additional feature such as Call Waiting or Answer Call per line

	Taxes (yes, the phone company will tax you for using their lines!)
▼ *Insurance*	Liability insurance is at least $200 a year or more depending upon the type of business and where it is located
▼ *Taxes*	Federal, State Tax, and for some States, Personal Property Taxes
▼ *Payroll*	Tax withholdings and all that goes along with it
▼ *Legal Fees*	Attorney, Accounting, Banking, and fees
▼ *Supplies*	Stationary & Business Cards Business Forms Copy paper, pens, (just go to your favorite office supply store!)
▼ *Equipment*	Furniture (decide if it is better to lease or purchase) Copier, Fax, Computers Telephone system Water cooler (if you don't like the water out of the faucet)! Coffee maker (if you or your customer drink coffee)
▼ *Memberships*	Books, Tapes, On-line Newsletters Newspaper Magazines & Periodical Trade & Business Organizations

Before you start this process, remember to:
    1. PRAY, ask those you trust for counsel,
    2. PRAY, ask those you trust for counsel, and
    3. PRAY!

Am I clear on this point?

BIBLICAL REFERENCE:

If God doesn't build the house, the builders only build shacks. If God doesn't guard the city, the night watchman might as well nap. It's useless to rise early and go to bed late, and work your fingers to the bone. Don't you know he enjoys giving rest to those he loves?

Psalm 127:1-2 The Message

SPIRITUAL PRINCIPLE #6
Counting The Cost (Are you able and capable of operating your own company?)

> *Decide not rashly.*
> *The decision made*
> *Can never be recalled*
>
> *Henry W. Longfellow*

DECISION TIME

BIBLICAL REFERENCE:
And whosoever doth not bear his cross, and come after me, cannot be my disciple. For which of you, intending to build a tower, sitteth not down first, and counteth the cost, whether he have sufficient to finish it? Lest haply, after he hath laid the foundation, and is not able to finish it, all that behold it begin to mock him, Saying, This man began to build, and was not able to finish.
Luke 14:27-30 KJV

Now is the time for you to consider everything you have read in this book and decide if the vision you have for a business idea is feasible. Does it make sense (and cents)? Is it a profitable enterprise or is it something you enjoy doing as a hobby. Listed below are ten questions for you to answer. The only answers that matter are your honest ones. This exercise is another part of *Counting The Cost*, or as some would say *"Put your money where your mouth is"*.

After completing this exercise you may realize that you are not totally prepared to start working on your business idea full time; if so, then I have done my job of arresting you from making a bad decision to quit your full-time job and plunge into something you are not ready for! Starting a business is risky and maintaining a profitable one can be even riskier. It is better to count the cost on this side and decide to wait, than to start down the road of entrepreneurship and fail. As the quote states, a decision made can **never** be recalled!

Take time to answer the following questions, even if it means you need a few days to complete them.

1. What do I enjoy doing?

2. Can I make a profit from it?

3. Will I dedicate the proper time, money and energy to consider what I enjoy: (select one)

▼ *A hobby?*
▼ *A sellable craft?*
▼ *A part-time job?*
▼ *A full time business/job/career/lifestyle?*

Why?

4. Is anybody else doing what I want to do?

5. If yes, how many companies in my geographical area?

6. What are the:

  ▼ *Similarities*

  ▼ *Differences*

7. Are they hiring anyone to fill a position that compares to what I want to do?
   If yes, what are the qualifications they look for in a person?

8. Can I talk to the owner to find out:

  ▼ *How they became successful in their business*
  ▼ *What are the pros and cons of the business/industry*
  ▼ *What did they do to get started*
  ▼ *How do they run their operations*
  ▼ *How difficult is it to keep the company going*
  ▼ *Words of wisdom and advice*

9. Have you adequately *counted the cost* for being in business full-time as a way of life?

10. Are you able to stand the emotional, mental and physical stress of being your own boss?

Quick decisions are unsafe decisions!
Sophocles Oedipus Tyrannus

BIBLICAL REFERENCE:
Anyone who won't shoulder his own cross and follow behind me can't be my disciple. Is there anyone here who, planning to build a new house, doesn't first sit down and figure the cost so you'll know if you can complete it? If you only get the foundation laid and then run out of money, you're going to look pretty foolish. Everyone passing by will poke fun at you: 'He started something he couldn't finish.'

Luke 14:27-30 The Message

SPIRITUAL PRINCIPLE #6
Counting The Cost (Are you able and capable to operate your own company)?

Your time is always ready time.
You are ready for every good work that comes your way.
To be of a ready mind is what you desire and
To be ready always to give an answer to every man that asks
You a reason of the hope that is in you with meekness is what God requires.
Carla A. Nelson
John 7:6; Titus 3:1; 1 Peter 5:2; 1 Peter 3:15

Are You Ready?

BIBLICAL REFERENCE:
Every purpose is established by counsel: and with good advice make war.
Proverbs 20:18 KJV

By now you have read much about what you need to do to keep company with God from the initial onset of your vision. I would like you to take the time to answer these questions to begin putting your thoughts in action.

1. Do you have a written plan to implement your business idea?

    a. If yes, are you on target with the timelines you set for the company?
    (Explain in detail)

b. If yes, what have you accomplished in your plan thus far and when was it completed? (No matter how small)

c. If no, why not?

2. Are you able to make major decisions on your own in a moment's notice?

3. Describe the latest encounter you had when a project did not go the way you planned.

a. How did you handle the situation?

b. Were you able to control your temper?

c. How did you get along with other people working on the project?

d. Were you able to overcome the obstacles, complete the project and satisfy your customer?

4. Do you want to start your business because you are tired of answering to someone else and you want to be your own boss?

   a. Do you realize that your customers become your boss?

   b. Do you realize that you will always answer to someone else?

   c. Do you have what it takes to be humble (remain calm under pressure)?

5. Do you have the ambition, boldness, courage, and determination to see your vision to start your business to the end?

6. Have you consulted with your Red Team?

7. Are you ready to be Committed, Focused, Patient, Persistent, Responsible, Silent, and Trusting as you implement your vision to start your business?

BIBILICAL REFERENCE:
Form your purpose by asking for counsel, then carry it out using all the help you can get.

Proverbs 20:18 The Message

RISKS

To laugh is - to risk appearing the fool.

To weap is – to risk appearing sentimental

To reach out for another is – to risk involvement

To expose feelings is – to risk exposing your true self

To place your ideas, your dreams before the crowd is – to risk their loss

To love is – to risk not being loved in return

To live is – to risk dying

To hope is – to risk despair

To try is – to risk failure

But risks must be taken, because the greatest hazard in life is to risk nothing.
The person who risks nothing, does nothing, has nothing and is nothing.
He may avoid suffering and sorrow, but he simply cannot learn, feel, change, grow, love, or live. Chained by his certitudes, he is a slave; he has forfeited freedom.

Only a person who RISKS is FREE!

Author Unknown

NOTES

SPIRITUAL PRINCIPLE #7
Business Fundamentals: Write The Vision Down (Doing first things first).

*More than half of all new businesses fail during their first two years
of operations.
More than 90% of all business fail within the first ten years.*
U.S. Small Business Administration Statistic

THE BASIC ESSENTIALS FOR A WINNING
BUSINESS PLAN

BIBLICAL REFERENCE:
*…Write the vision, and make it plain upon tables, that he may run that readeth
it. For the vision is yet for an appointed time, but at the end it shall speak, and
not lie: though it tarry, wait for it; because it will surely come, it will not tarry.
Behold, his soul which is lifted up is not upright in him: but the just shall live
by his faith.*
Habakkauk 2:2-4 KJV

Before you begin any project you must have a plan. The larger your project is, the more detailed your plan should be. So it is in the world of business. A *business plan* is an internal living, breathing document (as it grows up over time) that guides your company in the desired direction (path) you want it to go. The primary purpose of the *business plan* is to act as a blueprint of your house (company) for the founder, owners or partners, managers, and key employees to use on a daily basis. It is also used as a tool to raise capital with bankers, investors, suppliers and customers.

As you prepare your *business plan* carefully consider just how you are going to make your vision for business a successful company. You must decide who will be responsible for what and how each person carry out those responsibilities. You set the goals (milestones) to measure the effectiveness of your *business plan*. You guide the progress of your plan. If it is off target, you make the necessary adjustments to correct it.

Use your *business plan* as a blueprint and managing tool for your company to keep you prepared, committed, focused, patient, persistent, responsible, silent, trusting and headed in the right direction (path). If you do not compare your planned blueprint to the actual building of the house (company), you will not know if you are building a good house on a firm foundation. You will not know if you are headed in the right direction; the path God planned for you before the foundations of the world. The *business plan* describes your company and answers the famous six *W/H* questions:

> ▼ *Who you are*
> ▼ *What you do*
> ▼ *Where you are headed*
> ▼ *When you expect to get there*
> ▼ *How you expect to get there*
> ▼ *Why you will be successful*

Listed below are the basic components for any *business plan* you prepare for your company. There are many components to a *business plan* and the components may vary depending upon the industry or business you are entering, however there are some basic components for all plans. The seven reasons for writing a business plan are:

1. *To encourage you to be specific. Mental, informal, plans tend to be vague.*

2. *To evaluate the feasibility of your vision before you invest the time, energy and money into starting a company on a full time basis.*

3. *To visualize to others (paint a picture) of your vision (business idea).*

4. *To show the world you are serious about starting a business and building a company.*

5. *To guide the vision (business idea) on the right path.*

6. *To use as a business tool as you plan, market, and raise capital and grow.*

7. *To improve your opportunities for business success.*

Write down all the services or products your business can provide. If your potential customers cannot read or understand what you are selling they will not know or buy what you got! Be specific when writing your business plan. The rule of thumb is to write your plan in laymen's language so that the average ten-year-old will understand what you have to offer. Never use jargon or industry terms; do not assume your customers know what you do, so you must tell them what you do! Writing a business plan will help you achieve eight major steps toward success:

1. *Define your company goals and objectives.*

2. *Formulate your strategies to reach your goals and objectives.*

3. *Prioritize your goals and objectives.*

4. *Set the schedule and timetables for your goals and objectives.*

5. *Detail the activities and responsibilities of your company.*

6. *Identify the problems and offer solutions your company may encounter.*

7. *Improve the decision-making, efficiency and controls in your company.*

8. *Outline your financial needs and goals.*

NOTE: There are many reference books, CD ROM's, manuals and how-to guides on preparing a business plan. I offer an outline to a successful business plan based on the Seven Spiritual Principles you just learned. I always recommend that YOU write the business plan yourself then obtain assistance from your local small business development center, business institute, the U.S. Small Business Administration in your area. See *References* for detailed information.

As you write remember that you are building the foundation of your house – your company. (Once you get your company started, it will begin to feel like your house because of the amount of time and money you will spend on it. Believe me when I say this)! You will want your company to be strong and firm, build upon a Rock – the Rock of Jesus.

Pray for the wisdom, creativity and guidance from God. Make sure you have heard from God clearly about starting this business idea, especially when it is a fresh idea; something that no one else has done before. You may hesitate or *draw back* thinking that your business idea is inconceivable. God's word says in Hebrews 10:38 *that the just shall live by faith: but if any man draw back my soul (God) shall have no pleasure in him (you).* Besides, according to Matthew 1:26 what is impossible with man is possible with God. You have nothing to lose and everything to gain! It will not be easy but it is a done deal if you take the first step...***WRITE THE VISION DOWN!!!***

BIBLICAL REFERENCE:
Write this. Write what you see. Write it out in big block letters so that it can be read on the run. This vision-message is a witness pointing to what's coming. It aches for the coming – it can hardly wait! And it does not lie. If it seems slow in coming, wait. It's on its way. It will come right on time.
Habakkuk 2:2-3 The Message

SPIRITUAL PRINCIPLE #7
Business Fundamentals: Write The Vision Down (Doing first things first).

Some agreements are made with a handshake and some are made in blood.
Some agreements are made with a verbal word and some are
sealed with a kiss.
I think the best agreements are made with a written word.
Get It In Writing!

Carla A. Nelson

Legal Forms of Business Entities
Your Covenant

BIBLICAL REFERENCE:
I the LORD have called thee in righteousness, and will hold thine hand, and will keep thee, and give thee for a covenant of the people, for a light of the Gentiles; To open the blind eyes, to bring out the prisoners from the prison, and them that sit in darkness out of the prison house. I am the LORD: that is my name: and my glory will I not give to another, neither my praise to graven images. Behold, the former things are come to pass, and new things do I declare: before they spring forth I tell you of them.

Isaiah 43:6-9 KJV

Deciding what type of business structure you should chose for your company is vital to the growth and success of its future. The business structure or entity is like a *covenant* you are making with God, yourself, and to the business community you will serve. God is using you to fulfill His purpose. For this reason, consider yourself privileged and choose your business structure wisely.

It is important to carefully review the advantages, disadvantages, liability and income tax responsibilities before you chose. As your business grows you may be able to change from one entity to another. For example, if you begin your business as a Sole Proprietorship and want to change it to a Corporation once it begins to make money, you can do so by filing the required documents;

however, if you have a corporation and want to change it to a partnership, you may have to dissolve the company and start afresh.

1. SOLE PROPRIETORSHIP

▼ **Definition** - A business owned by one individual.

▼ **Income Taxes** – The business owner is taxed directly on the business income at the applicable individual rate. The business owner is responsible to pay all of the self-employment tax. The income or loss is reported and taxes paid on the owner's individual tax return.

▼ **Liability** – The business owner is personally responsible for all business liabilities. Creditors may ask for the owner to use personal assets to pay for business debts.

▼ **Costs** – Applicable license fees if necessary. Business name documents if it is different from the owner's name.

▼ **Advantages** – The business owner is solely responsible for the decisions and owns all the assets. The profits are taxed once and the tax rates are low. The organizational structure is simple and it is easy to dissolve.

▼ **Disadvantages** – There are no separate legal status between the individual and the business. The owner has unlimited personal liability. The owner is limited in raising operating capital.

2. PARTNERSHIP

▼ **Definition** – Created by an agreement (oral or written) among two or more partners. There are no maximums. The partners jointly own the assets used for the business activity. There are *General Partnerships* (all partners share the profits, losses, assets and liabilities) and there are *Limited Liability Partnerships* (must include at least one general partner and the limited partners do not risk personal liability other than their capital contributions).

▼ **Income Taxes** – The Partnership is not subject to income taxes. It files for informational purposes only. The income or loss is passed through the *General or Limited Partners* according to their proportionate shares. Each partner is taxed on their share of the income at their respective tax rate, regardless if the partner actually received the income or not. Partnership income is also subject to self-employment tax.

▼ **Liability** – *General Partners* are each personally responsible for all liabilities of the partnership. *Limited Partners* are not personally responsible for partnership liabilities. They are only at risk to the extent of their capital investment in the partnership.

▼ **Costs** – Attorney fees to draft and negotiate the partnership agreement. Filing fees for Limited Partnerships and for General Partnerships in some local jurisdictions.

▼ **Advantages** – Highly flexible and may be tailored to the special needs of each partner with few limitations. Profits and losses may be shared irregularly. Low individual tax rates and no double taxation.

▼ **Disadvantages** – *General Partnerships* have unlimited personal liability. *Limited Partnerships* can be complex, especially those that involve limited and corporate general partners. Complex tax rules apply when profits and losses are shared disproportionately.

3. CORPORATION

▼ **Definition** – A separate legal entity created by applicable state corporation laws. The corporation, commonly called a **C** Corporation, owns business assets and in turn is owned by the shareholders. It must have at least one shareholder and there is no maximum. Shareholders may be individuals, partnerships, trusts, or other corporations. Corporations can have common or preferred stock, and they can be open or closed corporations.

▼ **Income Taxes** – The Corporation is a tax-paying entity and pays taxes on its profits. Shareholders are taxed at their individual rate only when they receive dividends, thus causing a double taxation. Dividends are not subject to self-employment taxes. Losses are not passed through to the shareholder but may be carried forward to the next year to offset future income.

▼ **Liability** – Creditors may look to the assets of the corporation for payment but not at the shareholders' personal assets for payment; however most suppliers will require the CEO to sign a personal guarantee to ensure that payments will be made. When a corporation is involved in several business activities (ventures) it can form subsidiaries to protect the assets of one business activity from the liability of another.

▼ **Costs** – Legal fees for document preparation of the articles of incorporation, bylaws, corporate minutes, and if necessary, shareholder agreements.

▼ **Advantages** - Limited shareholder liability. Shareholders are not taxed until income is distributed to them. The Corporation can live on after the death of the owner.

▼ **Disadvantages** - Income is subject to double taxation (owner and company) while the losses cannot be passed to the owner. Annual Shareholders meetings are required and corporations can be heavily regulated through state and local laws.

4. S CORPORATION

▼ **Definition** – A more limited structure than a regular corporation. No more than 35 shareholders are permitted. All shareholders must be individuals and only one class of stock can be issued. All shareholders must be U.S. citizens.

▼ **Income Taxes** – An S Corporation does not pay federal taxes on its income. The income or loss is passed through to the shareholders. The S Corporation files information returns and each shareholder files a Form K-1 that reflects the shareholder's individual returns. Profits and losses are shared in proportion to the number of shares one has. Shareholders are taxed on their share of income whether or not it is distributed to them. Some states impose a tax on S Corporations at the corporate level.

▼ **Liability** – Same as a regular corporation except that subsidiaries are not allowed. If a shareholder wants to isolate liabilities one from another, they must create a new S Corporation. Under state law there is no difference between an S Corporation and a regular or C Corporation.

▼ **Costs** – Legal fees for document preparation of the articles of incorporation, bylaws, corporate minutes, and if necessary, shareholder agreements.

▼ **Advantages** – Limited liability, low individual tax rates. There is no double taxation.

▼ **Disadvantages** – Profits and losses cannot be shared disproportionately. There is limited flexibility in structuring ownership of providing individual preference when there is more than one shareholder.

5. LIMITED LIABILITY CORPORATION

▼ **Definition** – The Limited Liability Corporation, commonly called LLC, is a legal entity, which is separated from its owners, called members. The LLC, not the owners, own the business. There must be at least one member but there is no maximum. Usually there is one person designated as the registered agent.

▼ **Income Taxes** – the LLC may qualify to be treated exactly like a partnership for income purposes if properly structured. This way the company will be a pass-through entity, thus avoiding double taxation.

▼ **Liability** – The LLC is like the Corporation in that the members are usually not responsible for the debts of the business. Each member (professionals and other agents) is liable for their own negligence.

▼ **Costs** – Legal fees for preparing articles of organization and operating agreement and filing fees to organize.

▼ **Advantages** – Members have the same shield from liability as do corporate shareholders and have pure partnership tax treatment without the S Corporation type agreements.

▼ **Disadvantages** – There is no availability of tax-free fringe benefits that is provided by a C Corporation. Properly structuring the company can be difficult when there is more than one member. Not all states recognize them.

This information is only a general guide to help you understand the commonalties and differences of each business entity. I strongly advise you to spend time with your accountant and/or lawyer and any other member of your RED TEAM before choosing. If you do not have someone to help you decide you can always speak to a Small Business Development Center counselor or SCORE Representative in your area. I have listed their information under *Where To Go For More Information* in this section.

BIBLICAL REFERENCE:

I am God. I have called you to live right and well. I have taken responsibility for you, kept you safe. I have set you among my people to bind them to me, and provide you as a lighthouse to the nations, to make a start at brining people into the open, into light: opening blind eyes, releasing prisoners from dungeons, emptying the dark prisons. I am God. That's my name. I don't franchise my glory, don't endorse the no-god idols. Take note: The earlier predictions of judgment have been fulfilled. I'm announcing the new salvation work. Before it bursts on the scene, I'm tell you all about it.

Isaiah 43:6-9 The Message

SPIRITUAL PRINCIPLE #7
Business Fundamentals: Write The Vision Down (Doing first things first).

To write your Business Plan I suggest you use a Business Plan resource guide to assist you.
The resource guide can be in the form of a Book, CD-ROM, or an Internet Tool.
What is most important is that YOU must do your own Business Plan.
Carla A. Nelson

BIBLICAL REFERENCE:
Seest thou a man diligent in his business? He shall stand before kings; he shall not stand before mean men.
Proverbs 22:29 KJV

Your Company Name
Business Plan

Section I   **EXECUTIVE SUMMARY**

The Executive Summary is the most important part of the plan because it gives the reader a brief overview of the plan for your company. (It gives the reader a sense of how you will maintain your house). Consider the Executive Summary as the gateway to your company (the front door to your house). The banker or investor (invited guest) will read the Executive Summary first (determine how well they are greeted). If they like what they read (if the greeting is warm), they will flip to the end of your plan to read the Financial Plan and Analysis to see how you intend to manage your revenues (they will want to go into your kitchen to see how you prepare your meals).

If your financial plan makes sense (if your meals are well prepared), they will read the rest of the plan to determine if they should lend you money on behalf of their investors (they will stay for a good meal to determine how good you cook and tell others about your skills)!

The Executive Summary is comprised of the following:

▼ *Type of Business* – describe the legal entity of the company as listed in *References*

▼ *Company Information/Background* – section II

▼ *Products and Service Offerings* – section III

▼ *Marketing Analysis* – section IV

▼ *Marketing Plan* – section V

▼ *Management Owner Information* – section VI

▼ *Financial Plan and Analysis* – section VII

Section II COMPANY INFORMATION/BACKGROUND

This section describes the structure of the company. It explains to the reader in detail the Purpose, Vision and Goals, Mission and Vision Statement of the company. This is also the section where the history or concept of the company is listed. If you know where the company will be physically located that information will be listed here.

▼ *Vision & Mission Statement* – indicate the mission and vision of the company. Taken from *Creating Your Mission and Vision Statement* as listed in *Spiritual Principle #1*.

▼ *History* – explain the concept of your business idea. Taken from your *Purpose* and *Vision* for starting the company as listed in *Spiritual Principle #1*.

▼ *Business Goals* – explain the current status of the company, the products and services the company will offer, how you plan to expand the company and how you intend to make money. Taken from your *Goals* as listed in *Spiritual Principle #1*.

▼ *Legal Formation* – indicate the legal structure of the company. The legal structure you choose will determine what your legal, financial, and ethical obligations are to your customers, the public, the government, and the investors or shareholders of the company. Taken from your *Goals* as listed in *Spiritual Principle #1* and Legal Entities as listed in *References*.

▼ *Location & Facilities* – identify where the business will be located and a detailed physical description (concept design, square footage, and specialized equipment). If your company relies on foot traffic location is key. The business environment includes the demographics (population), geographic (urban or rural) and accessibility (methods of transportation) to the office or facility. Taken from your *Goals* as listed in *Spiritual Principle #1* and *Steps to Obtaining Office Space* in *Spiritual Principle #7*.

▼ *Financial Status Summary* – explain the overall current financial structure of your company. This includes owner equity (how much money you have invested in the company), investor contributions, outstanding loans or lines of credit, the number of employees you have or intend to have (if any) and the overall workforce experience. The details will be listed in the Financial Plan and Analysis. Taken from your *Goals* as listed in *Spiritual Principle #1* and *The Initial Investment* in *Spiritual Principle #6*.

Section IV   MARKETING ANALYSIS

This section describes your understanding of the market you intend to sell your goods and services to and identifies your customer base. You must demonstrate that you have the knowledge, skill and ability to sell your product by explaining the industry of your company, the ideal customer, your competitors, and the percentage of the market share you expect to capture as your company grows. Use the answers from *Decision Time and Are You Ready in Spiritual Principle #6* to assist you with this section.

▼ *Market Summary* – keep the summary brief and to the point. Discuss the strengths of the market and indicate the supporting documents (where you got your information). Describe your market in the positive tone to keep the reader interested.

▼ *Industry Analysis* – discuss the trends of your market. All industries have cycles and you must identify what they are for your company. It is also important to indicate what the market trends are nationally and locally. Identify any contributing factors that can influence your market trends positively or negatively such as the environment, government regulations and laws, or technical advancements.

▼ *Target Market* – identify the type of people and their characteristics you expect to have as your customer and why they will buy from you. Discuss how the product or service you provide is best suited for your potential customer based on their profile, demographics, geography, and the location of your company. Use the information gathered from *Your Support System* as listed in *Spiritual Principle #6* to assist you.

▼ *Customer Profile* – develop your customer profile based on the vision of who you wish to serve and the company's target market analysis. The profile consists of a customer's education level, economic status, gender, lifestyle, family status, and sometimes their spiritual affiliation. You must demonstrate that you understand their buying habits and show significant revenue to sustain the company over time.

▼ *Major Competitors & Participants* – identify who your competitors are and what makes your company different from theirs. Identify the portions of the market that are underserved or where no attention is given.

▼ *Projected Market Growth* – discuss how your company will grow during the next 12 months, five year and ten year mark. Indicate what the reasonable increase of your market share will be during these time periods, how the trends and cycles will affect your growth and the impact it will have on your customer.

Section III   PRODUCT & SERVICE OFFERINGS

This section describes the specific product or service your company will provide. Define what you are selling by describing its concept and methodology. Explain in detail the unique characteristics of the product or service and how it differs from the competition.

▼ *Products/Services Summary* – describes your product or service in general terms. Identify the components of your company that enhances your product or service such as personalized customer service, customization of the product or service, free training, repairs or warranties.

▼ *Detailed Description of Product/Service Line* – this is where you specifically describe each product or service you offer. The reader should have a clear understanding of its' purpose and how it differs from what your competitor offers.

▼ *Competition Comparisons* – almost every business industry has competitors. Your responsibility is to explain to the reader how your product or service does it better, faster, cheaper, or is more convenient. List the strengths and weaknesses of your product or service of your direct competitor (the same franchised restaurant) or an indirect competitor (a family owned restaurant). Indicate your plan to overcome those weaknesses such as location, hours of operation or experience in the industry.

▼ *Product/Service Uniqueness* – describe the distinguishing characteristics of the company such as speed or quality of service, price, design, variations, atmosphere, location, quality and quantity. Indicate the results of your test market group (potential customers) regarding their perception or value of the product or service.

▼ *Research & Development* – this is mostly for companies that manufacture a product. Technology advances the use of most products every 12-18 months; therefore, it is important to stay ahead of the competition. Indicate how your company develops or improves on the products you offer and the life cycle of that product.

▼ ***Patents & Trademarks (if applicable)*** – protected by the U.S. Government, Patents are official documents that give the owner exclusive control and possession of a new or unique product for a specific term of years. Trademarks are official documents that give the owner exclusive control and possession of a trade name, brand, proprietary information or intellectual property. Indicate the patent and/or trademark the company owns or are pending. See *References* for more detailed information.

Section V   MARKETING PLAN

This section describes in detail your strategy for getting your product or service to the marketplace through distribution, promotion, pricing, sales appeal, market penetration, and retention. It explains in detail the methods of communicating and attracting potential customer to your company.

▼ *The Message* –the purpose of your company is the first message you must create. The Mission and Vision Statements become your first message. Included in the message would be a brief description of your product and the target market that would buy what you are selling. You will also indicate the advertising vehicles you plan to use. Clearly identify and describe what you are selling to your customer.

▼ *Product/Service Pricing Strategy* – how you plan to be competitive in your market is answered in this section. You will need to determine if your prices will be below, at or above the average market rate for your product or service. Setting the price for services tend to be more difficult than it is for products. You will determine what works best for you based on the strategy you implement but don't be afraid to change if you find your strategy does not work for you.

▼ *Product Positioning* – positioning your product or service is how you intend to advertise or "present" what you sell to your target market group. In other words, how can you get the best bang for your buck? Have you noticed on television most household and feminine products are sold during the day when soap operas are on because studies show women watch television as they clean the house, and are the ones that make those purchases. Beverage and snack commercials are shown during sporting events because you must have something cold to drink and something to snack on during a good game.

▼ ***Promotional Strategy*** – another word for promotional strategy is sponsorship. You can advertise or promote your company by giving your money to an organization, event, sporting team, or place of worship to place your company name, logo and/or marketing materials at their event. Your message becomes twofold. You are indirectly selling your product or service as you let the public know that you are community minded, a corporate citizen, and concerned about others.

Section VI   MANAGEMENT & OWNER INFORMATION

This section describes those persons who have the responsibility of the daily operations for the company. List the various positions by title, the number of people needed per position and the necessary qualifications. The more experience your company possesses, the more favorable you are viewed by the reader, especially if it is a potential investor. It is also a good idea to include an organizational chart but it is not required.

▼ *Management Team* – these are the key people who will represent your company to your customers and suppliers. Their title could be President and Vice President; Chief Executive Officer (CEO), Chief Operating Officer (COO), and Chief Information Officer (CIO); or Executive Director, Deputy Director. The title may vary depending upon the structure of your company. Describe what their area of expertise is to the position they hold and how it benefits the company. Include a resume on each person listed. You would also indicate who your *Red Team* is as listed in *Spiritual Principle #7,* and see *References* for the definition of the titles listed.

▼ *Use of Consultants or Sub Contractors* – identify any consultant or sub contractor you will use on a continual basis and the work they are responsible to do. If you do not have specific names, the position held for a consultant that you could outsource work to (such as the Information Technology or Human Resources Dept.) or sub contractor (such as the Graphic Artist, Printer, or a Trainer).

▼ *Compensation* – indicate the salary, bonus, commission, and benefit plan such as profit sharing, pension, and company stock the management team will receive and the percentage increments over the years. To obtain and retain a good team you will have to pay them well and on time. Some companies might offer a lower salary than their competitors but the benefit package offered is much more attractive to the management team than the actual dollars. (This information should be listed in detail in

Section VII - the Financial Plan and Analysis of this sample plan). See References for a definition of terms.

▼ *Board of Directors* – list the people who guide the company to grow, direct and position the company to become profitable. If your company is not incorporated, you can call them your board of advisors. You need to indicate if the board is financially responsible should the company file for bankruptcy or is sued. Their resume should also be included in the plan.

Section VII   FINANCIAL PLAN & ANALYSIS

This section is the most important section of the entire plan. Remember I indicated that if the Executive Summary peaks their interest, in the next section the reader will turn to the Financial Plan and Analysis. You must be able to demonstrate the ability of your company to make money. It is not always expected that you will make a profit immediately. Some companies do not show a profit for five years; at the same time the company should not show dangerous losses either. The reader (prospective investor) will want to see how you plan to financially accomplish (sell) what you said you would do in the beginning of the *business plan*. You should always consult your accountant to prepare this section of your plan.

▼ *Initial Capital Requirements* – some people refer to this as your "Use of Funds" or "Start-up Budget". Indicate what the source of your initial investment is and where it came from. Detail what you spent the money on and if it is a loan request, indicate how you intend to spend the money once you receive it. The budget should include but is not limited to the following:

• Accounting Fees	• Advertisement/Media	• Equipment
• Furniture	• Improvements/ Repairs	• Income
• Insurance	• Lease Space	• Legal Fees
• Licenses/Permits	• Occupancy	• Professional Fees
• Promotional Fees	• Salaries & Wages	• Stationary
• Supplies	• Telephone	• Utilities

Refer to the section on *The Initial Investment* as listed in *Spiritual Principle #6.*

▼ *Cash Flow or Budget Statements* – some people refer to this as your "Operating Budget". This statement shows when you need more cash requirements to run the company. It may be for inventory due to an unexpected increase of sales or an increase of payroll, utilities, or other expenses. State what your monthly expenses will be to show if and when you expect an increase of supplies and/or cash. Specify what your monthly budget will be for the next 12 months by month, then for the next 3-5 years. The Cash Flow budget should include but not be limited to the following:

- Accounting Fees
- Advertisement/Media
- Depreciation on Assets
- Dues/Subscription Fees
- Insurance
- Inventory/ Raw Materials
- Lease Space/Rent
- Legal Fees
- Loan Payments
- Maintenance/Repairs
- Miscellaneous Expenses
- Payroll Expenses
- Personnel
- Professional Fees
- Promotional Fees
- Rent on Office Space
- Salaries & Wages
- Supplies
- Taxes
- Telephone
- Utilities

▼ *Projection Statements* –this statement shows the financial productivity and profitability of your company's operation, through the value of your capital equity, assets, liabilities and liquidity of your company for the given planning period. It gives the reader an indication of how you plan to make money for the next 12 months to five years. You should prepare a statement for the first 12 months by month, then a statement for the next 3-5 years. Remember these are projections, changes will occur as your company grows and that is where the *actual* Income Statements and Balance Sheets are needed.

   a) *Income Statement* – also referred to as your profit and loss statement, this is a financial document that shows the income and expenses of the company over a given period of time. In other words, how much money you have left after all your expenses are paid. It shows the Revenue (sales, cost of sales and gross profit) from the Expenses (administrative and general, before taxes). When taxes are deducted, that figure becomes your net profit.

   b) *Balance Sheet* – also referred to as an equity statement, is a financial document that shows the assets and liabilities of the company over a given period of time. In other words, the net worth of the company. It is made up of Assets that are *fixed* - (equipment, furniture, building or land, something that can be depreciated at least for five years or more) and *current* (cash on hand, account receivables, inventory and prepaid expenses, something that can be easily liquidated).

Liabilities that are *current* - (something due to be paid in the next 12 months, accrued expenses, taxes, or short term notes) and *long-term debt* (equipment leases longer than 12 months, accounts payable, loans and lines of credit). The balance between the assets and liabilities is the equity you have in the company.

Do not be surprised if it is negative for a few years. It is normal to show a negative statement after the first 12 months but it should decrease each year and show some kind of profit before or around year five. This is particularly true if you leased much of your equipment or furniture or borrowed money to get started. Two things I suggest you steer clear of until the company begins to show a profit.

▼ *Break Even Analysis* – this formula is used to calculate the point at which your company will begin to even out its revenues to expenses, thus the term *break even*. The analysis tells you how much revenue in gross sales you will need to meet all of your expenses on a consistent basis or if you will have enough revenue to continue business operations. The formula is given in *Calculating Business Income as listed in Spiritual Principle #6.*

▼ *Exist Strategy* – indicate what the future plans are for the company, whether it is to sell it to a larger company, take the company public, pass it down to your heir, or dissolve it once the mission (purpose) is completed. This strategy should also include what will be done if the company does not show a profit over a set time. (How far will you go before you bail out?). Refer to *the Mission and Vision Statements as listed in Spiritual Principle #1* and *Your Personal Life as listed in Spiritual Principle #6.*

BIBLICAL REFERENCE:
Observe people who are good at their work – skilled workers are always in demand and admired; they don't take a back seat to anyone.

Proverbs 22:29 The Message

NOTES

SUMMARY

It Is An Honor And A Privilege To Bless You!

I am honored that God would use me to be a blessing to you by writing this book. Major moves in my life tend to appear to me first in my dreams. As a child I always had vivid and colorful dreams that caused me to ask my mother why I was born and question what was life all about. As a woman I have learned to embrace my dreams as visions from the Lord as He shows me why I was born and answers my questions to the meaning of life. My dreams allow me to visualize what is forthcoming in my life while Holy Spirit comforts me through my journey. This book idea was a *vision* and a *major move* in my life that took seven years to come to fruition.

This book was not easy nor difficult to write, it was *awkward!* To put into words what I want to convey to you about the Lord being your guide and Holy Spirit being your comforter in your business is a new concept. It was awkward mainly because it took me a few years to realize a measure of success in my own business. It is through those I have come to learned that success is not measured by how much money you have at your disposal (notice, I did not say *in the bank*), but *true success* is measured by the goals you are able to accomplish and how your vision makes a positive influence in another person's life. Affecting the lives of others to do their best in business is *my passion,* how I do it is *my process*!

Having this kind of affect on someone's life can be hard to measure without the constant feedback from those I have touched (*So let me know*)! My goal and prayer is that this book will have a positive influence in your life and add real value to your business idea! We live in a time where the world of business and politics are seeking answers from wise men and women of God to the questions of society's problems. As kingdom citizens we have the answers and we must begin to move from preaching the *Gospel of Endurance* to teaching the *Gospel of Dominion* in order to take back our rightful place in the earth. This book is just the beginning!

Elder Carla A. Nelson

REFERENCE:
The information, places and resources you can use in starting your company!

BIBLICAL REFERENCES IN REVIEW

Spiritual Principle Bible References In Order of Their Use

Purpose
- *Isaiah 4:8-11*
- *Romans 8:28-34*

Vision
- *Habakkuk 2:1-3*
- *Psalm 89:19*

Goals
- *Isaiah 55:6-11*
- *Philippians 3-13-14*

Creating Your Mission & Vision Statements
- *Biblical Reference – Luke 4:43*

Faith
- *Luke 12:22-31*
- *Romans 12:11-13*
- *1 Chronicles 29:19*
- *Psalm 138:7-8*
- *Psalm 75:5-6*
- *Psalm 31:23*
- *Mark 11:24*
- *Hebrews 10:38*
- *Proverbs 4:23*

Prayer
- *Mark 11:23-26*
- *Genesis 4:25-26*
- *Jeremiah 33:2-3*
- *1 John 5:14-15*
- *Psalm 91:11-12*
- *Nehemiah 1:11*
- *Philippians 4:4-7*
- *Luke 11:1-2, 9-10*
- *Mark 11:23-24*
- *Mark 16:17*
- *John 16:23-24*
- *Acts 2:1-5*
- *1 Chronicles 14-1-2, 13-15*

Preparation
- *Ecclesiastes 3:1, 9-14*
- *Proverbs 8:21*
- *Isaiah 48:17*
- *Proverbs 16:1-2*

Committed
- *Proverbs 16:3-4*
- *Genesis 39:8,22*

Focused
- *Proverbs 4:23-27*
- *Joshua 1:8*
- *Psalm 1:2-3*
- *Psalm 16:11*
- *Psalm 119:35,105-106*
- *Psalm 139:3*
- *Proverbs 4:18*
- *Matthew 3:16-17*
- *Matthew 4:19-20*
- *Matthew 21:2-3*

Patient
- *Ecclesiastes 7:7-10*
- *Psalm 40:1-2*
- *James 1:2-4*

Persistent
- *Luke 18:1-8*
- *Genesis Chapter 28-30*
- *Daniel Chapter 3*
- *Daniel Chapter 6*
- *Nehemiah Chapter 4*
- *The Book of Acts*

Responsible
- *Hebrews 13:15-17*
- *Luke 16:1-4, 8-13*

Silent
- *Psalm 28:1-2*
- *Psalm 94:16-18*

Trusting
- *Jeremiah 17:7-8*
- *Proverbs 3:5-6*

You Are The Business
- *Proverbs 22:29*
- *Galatians 5:22-23*
- *James 3:17-18*
- *John 4:31-38*
- *Galatians 6:8-9*
- *Matthew 25:1-13*
- *Nehemiah 4:19-22*
- *Acts 16:10-11*
- *Matthew 14:16-21*

The Good Steward
- *Luke 12:42-44*

Planning
- *Proverbs 19:20-21*
- *Proverbs 16:1-9*
- *Proverbs 2:1-11*

What's Under Your Ground?
- *Luke 6:47-49*
- *1 John 15:1-5*

Appearance Matters
- *Ephesians 6:10-18*
- *Nehemiah 4:15-18*
- *Matthew 4:1-11, 16-17*
- *2 Thessalonians 1:6-7*
- *Psalm 103:20-21*
- *Psalm 34:6-8*
- *Daniel 3:28*
- *1 Kings 19:4-8*
- *Psalm 91:11-12*
- *Matthew 26:53*

Your Personal Life
- *Proverbs 6:6-11*

The Red Team
- *Proverbs 15:22*

Steps To Obtaining Office Space
- *Psalm 127:1-2*

Decision Time
- *Luke 14:27-30*

Are You Ready?
- *Proverbs 20:18*

Basic Essentials For A Winning Business Plan
- *Habakkuk 2:2-4*

Legal Forms Of Business Entities:
- *Isaiah 43:6-9*

Sample Business Plan
- *Proverbs 22:29*

PROTECTING YOUR ORIGINAL IDEAS

▼ *Copyright* © - is a form of protection provided the authors of "original works of authorship" including literary, dramatic, musical, artistic, and certain other intellectual works. This protection is available to both published and unpublished works. They can also overlap with patents. www.copyright.gov

▼ *Patent* - is the grant of a property right to the inventor(s). The right conferred by the patent grant is, in the language of the statute and of the grant itself, "the right to exclude others from making, using, offering for sale, or selling" the invention in the United States or "importing" the invention into the United States. www.uspto.gov. There are three types of Patents:

Utility - anyone who invents or discovers any new and useful process, machine, article of manufacture, or compositions of matters, or any new useful improvement thereof.

Design - anyone who invents a new, original, and ornamental design for an article of manufacture.

Plant - anyone who invents or discovers and asexually repro-duces any distinct and new variety of plant.

▼ *Registration mark* ® - You can establish rights in a mark based on legitimate use of the mark. However, owning a federal trade-mark registration on the Principal Register provides several advantages, e.g., constructive notice to the public of the regis-trant's claim of ownership of the mark; a legal presumption of the registrant's ownership of the mark and the registrant's exclusive right to use the mark nationwide on or in connection with the goods and/or services listed in the registration; the ability to bring an action concerning the mark in federal court; the use of the U.S registration as a basis to obtain registration in foreign countries; and the ability to file the U.S. registration with the U.S. Customs Service to prevent importation of infringing foreign goods. www.ustpo.gov

▼ *Trademark*™ - is a word, phrase, symbol or design (logo), or a combination of words, phrases, symbols or designs, that identifies and distinguishes the source of the goods of one party from those of others.

▼ *Service Mark*^SM - is the same as a trademark, except that it identifies and distinguishes the source of a service rather than a product. The terms "trademark" and "mark" refer to both trademarks and service marks.

NOTE: Any time you claim rights in a mark, you may use the "TM" (trademark) or "SM" (service mark) designation to alert the public to your claim, regardless of whether you have filed an application with the United States Patent and Trade Office (USPTO). However, you may use the federal registration symbol "®" **only** after the USPTO actually *registers a mark*, and **not** while an application is pending. Also, you may use the registration symbol with the mark only on or in connection with the goods and/or services listed in the federal trademark registration.

▼ *Intellectual or Proprietary Property* – are use for Patent, Trademark, Copyrights and Related Rights, Trade Secrets, Technology, Education, Geographical Indications, Industrial Designs, Layout-Designs (Topographies) of Integrated, Protection of Undisclosed Information, Control of Anti-Competitive Practices in Contractual Licenses.

Information obtained from federal government web sites.

REFERENCES:
The information, places and resources you can use in starting your company!

PREFERRED BUSINESS BOOK LIBRARY

<u>**The 7 Habits of Highly Effective People**</u>: Powerful Lessons in Personal Change, *Covey, Stephen R.*, Simon & Schuster, Inc, 1990

<u>**The Art of Closing Any Deal**</u>: How to be a "Master Closer" in Everything You Do, *Pickens, James W.*, Warner Books, Inc., 1991

<u>**Becoming a Leader**</u>: Everyone Can Do It, *Munroe, Myles*, Pneuma Life, 1993

<u>**Built On Trust:**</u> Gaining The Competitive Advantage In Any Organization, *Ciancutti, MD, Arky & Steding, PhD, Thomas L.*, Contemporary Books, 2001

<u>**The Entrepreneur's Guide to Business Law**</u>, *Bagley, Constance E., Dauchy, Craig E.*, West Educational Publishing Company, 1998

<u>**Failing Forward:**</u> Turning Mistakes Into Stepping Stones For Success, John C. Maxwell,
Thomas Nelson Publishers, 2000

<u>**The Fifth Discipline**</u>: The Art & Practice of The Learning Organization, *Senge, Peter M.*, Doubleday Dell Publishing Group, Inc., 1990

<u>**First Things First**</u>, *Covey, Stephen R., Merrill, A. Roger, Merrill, Rebecca R.*, Simon & Schuster Inc., 1994

<u>**Getting to YES**</u>: Negotiating Agreement Without Giving In, *Fisher, Roger, Ury, William*, A Penguin Book, 1983

Guerrilla Marketing Weapons: 100 Affordable Marketing Methods For Maximizing Profits From Your Small Business, *Levinson, Jay Conrad*, Penuin Group, 1990

Jesus CEO: Using Ancient Wisdom for Visionary Leadership, *Jones, Laurie Beth*, Hyperion, 1995

Million Dollar Consulting: The Professional's Guide To Growing A Practice, *Weiss, Alan*, McGraw Hill, 1976 (Third Printing 2003)

The Millionaire Next Door, *Stanley, Ph.D., Thomas J., Danko, Ph.D., William D.*, Pocket Books, 1996

The Path: Creating Your Mission Statement for Work and for Life, *Jones, Laurie Beth*, Hyperion, 1996

The Personal Touch: What You Really Need to Succeed in Today's Business World, *Williams, Terrie*, Warner Books, 1994

Releasing Your Potential: Exposing The Hidden You, *Munroe, Myles*, Destiny Image, Inc., 1992

Race For Success: The Ten Best Opportunities for Blacks in America, *Fraser, George C.*, Avon Books, Inc., 1998

Smart Guide: to Managing Your Time, *Rogak, Lisa*, John Wiley & Sons, Inc., 1999.

Smart Movers: 14 Steps to Keep Any Boss Happy, 8 Ways to Start Meetings on Time, and 1600 More Tips to Get the Best from Yourself and the People Around You, *Deep, Sam, Sussman, Lyle*, Addison-Wesley Publishing Co., Inc., 1990

Smart Movers for People in Charge, *Deep, Sam, Sussman, Lyle*, Addison-Wesley Publishing Co., Inc., 1995

Start Smart Your Business Series: The #1 Resource for Starting Your Business, *PSI Research, Inc.*, The Oasis Press, 1998.

Success Runs in Our Race: The Complete Guide to Effective Networking in the African-American Community, *Fraser, George*, William Morrow & Company, Inc., 1994

The Think & Grow Rich Action Pack, *Hill, Napoleon*, Plume, 1990

The Truth About Money, *Edelman, Ric*, Georgetown University Press, 1996

Understanding The Purpose and Power of PRAYER: Earthy License for Heavenly Interference, *Dr. Munroe, Myles*, Whitaker House, 2002

Understanding Your Potential: Discovering The Hidden You, *Munroe, Myles*, Destiny Image, Inc., 1991

Unstoppable: 45 Powerful Stories of Perseverance and Triumph from People Just Like You, *Kersey, Cynthia*, Sourcebooks, Inc., 1998

The World's Best Known Marketing Secret: Building Your Business with Word-of-Mouth Marketing, *Misner, Ph.D., Ivan R.*, Bard Press, 1994

Yes, You Can! *Deep, Sam, Sussman, Lyle*, Addison-Wesley Publishing Co., 1996

REFERENCES:
The information, places and resources you can use in starting your company!

WHERE TO GO FOR MORE INFORMATION

▼ *Chambers of Commerce* – An organization to meet local, state and federal political officials, government agencies, and presidents of large and small companies. It is also where you learn and get involved in your business community. If you are of a particular ethnicity or sell your goods to a particular cultural market, joining that particular chamber is also a good idea. Look in your local phone book for the address, telephone number and web address for the nearest Chamber of Commerce in your area.

- *U.S. Chamber of Commerce*
  1615 H Street, NW
  Washington, DC 20062
  202-659-6000
  www.uschamber.com

- *Asian Chamber of Commerce*
  1219 East Glendale Avenue
  #25
  Phoenix, AZ 85020
  602-222-2009
  602-870-7562
  www.asianchamber.org

- *National Black Chamber of Commerce*
  1350 Connecticut Avenue, NW
  Suite 825
  Washington, DC 20036
  202-466-6888
  202-466-4918
  www.nationalbcc.org

- *United States Hispanic Chamber of Commerce*
  2175 K Street, NW
  Suite 100
  Washington, DC 20037
  202-842-1212
  202-842-3221
  www.ushcc.com

- *International Chamber of Commerce*
  38 Cours Albert ler
  75008 Paris, France
  +33 1 49 53 28 28
  +33 1 49 53 28 59

▼ *The Federal Citizens Information Center (FCIC)* - Supported by the United States General Services Administration, the FCIC has information on any subject you can think of from education and health, frauds and scams to Starting a Business, contacting your House Representative, Senator or the Office of the President. You can review or download the information you found or have it mailed to you for $0.50! Catalogs are also available for the asking.
  PO Box 100
  Pueblo, CO 81002
  1-800-Fed-Info
  www.pueblo.gsa.gov

▼ *Internal Revenue Service (IRS)*- Housed by the Department of the Treasury, the mission of The Internal Revenue Service is the nation's tax collection agency and administers the Internal Revenue Code enacted by Congress. Its mission: to provide America's taxpayers with top quality service by helping them understand and meet their tax responsibilities and by applying the tax law with integrity and fairness to all. The web site provides information and forms for individuals, businesses, churches, government entities and non-profit organizations. The web site does not provide tax related questions and answers. You can apply on line to obtain your Employer Identification Number (EIN) form to register.

Locate your local IRS office and telephone number in the telephone book or through this web site. www.irs.gov

▼ *National Minority Supplier Development Council (NMSDC) -* Providing a direct link between corporate America and minority owned businesses is the primary objective of the National Minority Supplier Development Council, one of the country's leading business membership organizations. It was chartered in 1972 to provide increased procurement and business opportunities for minority businesses of all sizes.

1040 Avenue of the Americas
Second Floor
New York, NY 10018
212-944-2430
212-719-9611
www.nmsdc.org

▼ *Psi Research, Inc.* - The leading publisher of small business information for over 25 years. The most diverse and comprehensive business libraries available dedicated to helping businesses start and grow.

P.O. Box 3727
Central Point, Oregon 97502
1-800-228-2275
www.psi-research.com

▼ *Service Corps of Retired Executives (SCORE) -* A resource partner to the Small Business Administration is dedicated to aiding to the formation, growth and success of small business nationwide. There are over 11,500 retired and active small business owners, executives and professionals willing to work with you to make confident business decisions an provide with reliable support. It's like having your own dedicated mentor on call. You can get fast, free and confidential email counseling at over 389 local chapters in the U.S.

SCORE Association
409 3rd Street, S.W.
6th Floor
Washington, DC 20024
1-800/634-0245
www.score.org

▼ **Quick Books Pro** - a software system to track THE MONEY!
1-800-330-2052
www.quickbooks.com

▼ **U.S. Department of Agriculture** - offers programs on entrepreneurship and publications on selling to the department both foreign and domestic.

1400 Independence Avenue
Washington, DC 20250
www.usda.gov

▼ **U.S. Department of Commerce** – listing of business opportunities available in the federal government both domestic and foreign.

Office of Business Liaison – Business Assistance Center
14th Street & Constitution Avenues, NW
Washington, DC 20230
www.commerce.gov

▼ **U.S. General Services Administration** - listing of everything the federal government agency buys.

18th & F Streets, NW
Washington, DC 20405
www.gsa.gov

▼ *U.S. Small Business Administration (SBA)* - this government
agency provides assistance to businesses.
> 409 3rd Street S.W.
> Washington, D.C. 20416
> Phone: 1-800-U-ASK-SBA
> www.sba.gov

▼ *The Coaching Group, LLC* - The Coaching Group focuses on
working with managers
who recognize the need for additional input into their corporate
strategy and business development initiatives. Their team guides
these managers step-by-step to institute change and produce quan-
tifiable results.
> Joshua I. Smith, Chairman and Managing Partner
> 600 14th Street, NW
> Suite 800
> Washington, DC 20005
> jsmith@coachinggrp.com

▼ *Other Business References, Government agencies and
Organizations to join*
- Community Groups (Civic or Homeowner groups)
- Industry/Trade Associations (Contractors, Hospitality, Retail,
  Trainers, etc)
- Libraries/Book Stores (Local, Universities, Internet)
- Professional Organizations (Accountants, Doctors, Engineers,
  Lawyers, etc.)
- Social Organizations (Fraternities, Sororities, and other non-
  profit organizations)
- State Agency for Business and Economic Development
- State Agency for Assessments and Taxation
- State Agency for Workforce and Training Division

INDEX

THANKS and APPRECIATIONS

My Mother

Dorothea B. Jordan, for giving birth to the Visionary and becoming my best cheerleader! Thank you for being my life-giver, sustainer, nurturer, defender, rock and comforter. It is because of you I am able to live, love and laugh. Your little girl is still dancing at the door because of you!

My Editors

Mrs. Barbara Davis, a quiet yet stately woman who I have admired from afar. Thank you for being one of my midwives. It is because of your skills this book is now healthy. Get ready because I have more babies on the way!

Elder Brenda J. Haliburton, you started out as a stranger to me and prayed to get me out of my part time cashiers position at a local grocery store. You prayed for me to be a successful entrepreneur, and came to volunteer your time to work for me. You are now my confidant because you pray for me to do everything God has purposed me to do in His Kingdom. You are my friend!

Mrs. Shelly-Gross Wade, you have always been an inspiration to me in business and you are a true example of a virtuous woman of God. Your quiet demeanor during your storms speaks volumes of wisdom and grace to me and those around you!

My Designer

Mr. Cecil Brathwaite, you always make me look good in pictures! Thank you for your words of encouragement, especially during the early years of my business. I am grateful for our friendship over the last decade.

Ms. Shalonda Moses, your creativity is truly a gift from God and part of your purpose in life. Continue to be the blessing that you are as you seek, pursue and subdue your vision!

My Family   *To those who did not understand what I was doing but supported me anyway and never judged me. To those who chose not want to understand, you made me stronger and more determined than I ever thought I could be!*

My Friends   *Both old and new, personal and professional. Your encouragement was needed more than you will ever know. I am grateful for your listening ears, watchful eyes and receptive hearts. Most of all I am grateful for your shoulders to cry on!*

My Supporters   *David Alston, Andrea Bedenbaugh, Kelvin Boston, Darlene Butts, Tammy Douglas, Bradley Farrar, Joaney Gore, Ron Hudson, D. Michael Lyles, Craig Muckle, Jeffrey Penn, Pastor Leon Lutete, Karen Peppins, Moshe "Blake" Powers, Katheryn Robinson, Joshua Smith, and Elder Paku Tshambu.*

My Initiator   *Dr. Myles Munroe, for your life and the boldness you have to teach The Kingdom of God Principles for Life. For the empowered life you gave to Dr. Charles Phillips so many years ago, who then gave empowered life to me. It is now time for me to give empowered life to others. Know that your life will live beyond your years on earth.*

My Motivator   *Dr. Charles Phillips who was a part of my original vision to "HEAL GOD'S PEOPLE THROUGH ECONOMIC MEANS. Who knew then that a decade later we would be here! Thank you for being in the place called THERE for me when I needed it most. You have been my mentor, coach, encourager, counselor, teacher, and even a father when mine left to be with the Lord. You never gave up on me or the VISION. When I did not understand what was happening to me or wanted to give up on my company, you reminded me of my vision and purpose for being born! That is what a true Pastor is all about!*

Printed in the United States
22531LVS00004B/110

9 781591 607946